I0135183

Self and Spirit

OTHER WORKS
BY ROBERT BOLTON

The Order of the Ages:
(World History in the Light of a Universal Cosmogony)

Keys of Gnosis

The One and the Many

Foundations of Free Will

Person, Soul, and Identity

Robert Bolton

Self and Spirit

First published in the USA
Sophia Perennis, 2005
Angelico Press/Sophia Perennis edition, 2024

Series editor: James R. Wetmore

For information, address:
Angelico Press,
169 Monitor St.
Brooklyn, NY 11222
angelicopress.com

ISBN 978-1-59731-056-7 (pb)
ISBN 978-1-59731-057-4 (cloth)

Cover design: Michael Schrauzer

CONTENTS

5

Self and Initiation: Conflicting Ideas

6

Platonism in Christianity

7

The Soul and Salvation

8

Conditions for Mystical Union

9
Life, Death, and Resurrection

Acknowledgments

Chapters 1, 2, 3, 6, 7, and 9 were originally published, prior to some additions and revisions, in *Sacred Web,* with titles as follows: chapter 1, first printed in *Sacred Web 5* as 'Reflections on the Stone'; chapter 2 first printed in *Sacred Web 4* as 'Dualism and the Philosophy of the Soul'; chapter 3 first printed in *Sacred Web 2* as 'The Ternary and the Quaternary'; chapter 6 first printed in *Sacred Web 10* as 'The Role of Platonism in Christianity'; chapter 7 first printed in *Sacred Web 15* as 'The Soul and Salvation'; chapter 9 first printed in *Sacred Web 7* as 'Life, Death, and Resurrection'.

Introduction

The reflections on the nature of the self in the following chapters have a close connection with the work of René Guénon and Frithjof Schuon, with the purpose of rethinking their vital idea of intellectual transcendence and of the role of intellectuality as a form of grace. For Guénon and Schuon the metaphysical core of religion is always a form of Hinduism, which they accept dogmatically as an expression of a primordial tradition, to which all the religions known to us are somehow affiliated. They assume that the Hindu wisdom as interpreted by Shankara is the medium in which the different traditions are reconciled, because of the numerous correspondences between it and them. I differ from this position for two reasons: firstly, because the central position of some Hindu doctrines among the religions can be explained on a very different basis, because its character as we know it has evolved through successive adaptations, notably to Buddhism, Christianity, and Islam. Secondly, because there is an opposition between Hinduism and Christianity which could be deep enough to remain even if all other religious differences were reconciled, not least where the Divine Logos is concerned.

Such are the problems occasioned by the idea that one religion can be the key to all the others, and for this reason, the unifying principle is best sought outside any actual religions, in a realm of first principles. The need is for a metaphysical basis for religious teachings which does not require the denial of anything essential to any one religion in particular. Any such answer must include some proof that the self is a reality in its own right, and not just a collective name for a succession of more or less related phenomena with no integrating principle. (Such a conclusion clearly appears in a curious agreement between much modern Non-Dualism and modern analytical philosophy in regard to the unreality of personality.)

The importance of this is far from being merely of personal interest, because all metaphysics and religion would be reduced to nothing if the self were not an objective reality. This is in fact the conclusion drawn by Empiricism with its disproof of the reality of the self, given by philosophers such as Hume.

Inevitably, proof of the reality of the self begins with a certain circularity; by treating it as a reality in the first instance, the justification for this can be found from the coherence of the conclusions deduced about it. In the general case, coherence alone would not be enough, since this could still fail the test of correspondence with the real, but with a universally comprehensive reality like the self, coherence is decisive. It is, moreover, the only foundation for whatever can be said about God, which is why Hume attacked it.

The main problem with knowledge of the self lies in the number of different levels on which the question 'What am I?' can be asked. The internal diversity of the self ranges from the most strictly individual to the most universal objects of knowledge, and even though they are all in continual interaction, knowledge on one level does not guarantee knowledge on any other. For psychology, the task is to understand the peculiarities of the individual, and to judge how far they reveal mental health or sickness, but these individual attributes are relative to elements which are common to all rational beings and which form the common center of all their faculties.

This primary core of conscious being is the subject of what follows, and I trace its properties through a number of subjects, which include that of salvation, because the true nature of a being cannot be understood without a knowledge of its last ends. The very question as to whether or not salvation is a possibility for the self makes a fundamental difference to what we think the self is.

The pupil of the eye performs a function on the physical level which aptly symbolizes that of the self, inasmuch as the latter is the nexus through which all experience and all kinds of knowledge must pass. None of the contents of experience can be unaffected by this relation, since things received always take on the qualities of the receiver, here including his qualities as a member of a species, and as an individual. For this reason, misunderstandings of the self lead to misunderstandings of everything else. First among the nonsenses caused by misunderstanding the self is the belief that one's own experiences and those of other people are all *caused by the world as it appears to oneself.* It will be explained in the first two chapters how the world as it appears to oneself is rather the end-product of a causal sequence, not the initiator of one, so that the objective world is not experienced directly, but is in a sense refracted, through the faculties of innumerable very different beings, and the grand total of all these reconstructions of the world go to make up what we should truly mean by 'the world'.[1]

If all our experiences are believed to be caused by the world as we perceive it, religion and mysticism on the one hand, and the natural sciences on the other will appear to fill all conceivable possibilities, none of them being able to convey any meaning for the role of the individual as such. This situation, in which the non-sensory basis of experience is not recognized, gives rise to the widespread delusion that the self must ultimately reduce either to just organic matter or to God, when in fact there is no need for it to be either. This is confirmed by the fact that the art of self-knowledge, where it is more than psychological, is at an all-time low today. Thus one ignores the fact that philosophy has always been able to reveal the third force by which the above extremes are balanced and contained.

Exoteric religion, however sincere, allows people to go on believing themselves to be solely what they appear to be to other people. Deeper insights into the self lead outside the exoteric, and are usually resisted in a mistaken belief that this must be a danger to orthodoxy. As C.G. Jung has put it, the failure to appreciate this has resulted in people who are devout 'to the point of stigmatization' without for all that realizing the nature of their inner being.

To resolve such paradoxes will require some explanation as to how the soul or self is in one way equal to the universe, while in another way that it is the smallest of the small points on which great matters turn. Whatever we know is thus only one-half of the real issue; the other is the fact that we know it. The grounds for this conception are explained further in terms of the *logos*-function in Chapter 6. Much of what is said about the nature of the self in Chapters 1

1. See Stephen Clark, *A Parliament of Souls*, p26 (Oxford: OUP, 1990).

and 2 is supported by post-Renaissance philosophies, but this does not mean any deviation from traditional wisdom, because they are used only for the ways in which they reveal the most essential ideas embodied in tradition. What is deduced about the self is thus fully in accord with the traditional teaching that each person is formed according to the world's many levels of being.

This conception is followed in Chapter 3 by an account of the self in terms of its most universal functions, these being cosmic and spiritual at once. This results from the way in which the soul links the body and the intellect; the fact that the person is formed in this way means that he has the potentiality to mediate between the natural and the supernatural. The realization of this cosmic role is dependent on the full development of free will, of which an account is given in Chapter 4.

How much this development may depend on initiation is considered in Chapter 5, in connection with what René Guénon says about it in his *Initiation and Spiritual Realization*. The criticisms and qualifications offered there are an approach to the ideas involved as far as they are amenable to philosophy; they would be less applicable to the overall spiritual intention of the book and the mystically inspirational side of Guénon. In strictly rational terms, his idea of salvation is problematic, because the salvific processes he speaks of could be interactions between real agents, in which case the individual person would be real, despite the exclusive reality attributed to the Principle or Self. On the other hand, if the individual is not real, no real events are taking place, and the relations concerned would be simply verbal; and in this case, in whom or in what would the spiritual transformations be taking place?

This indicates that something more than the purely intellectual is involved, which is not surprising, since the role of sentiment can never be eliminated, for the basic reason that the intellect can never work in separation from the will. Traditional forms of philosophy make this clear, but for some reason Guénon did not see this. Purity, or purification, when applied to the higher values, has a large element of the negative about it because it always requires the elimination or the exclusion of something. Consequently, a passion for purification, taken to an extreme and not balanced by any equal principle, will end by eliminating everything, including the things one wanted to purify. Traditionalist thought must avoid this if it is to be free from modern reductionism.

The universal role of Platonic metaphysics in Christianity and most other religions is considered in Chapter 6, and this role involves the *logos*-function which is the basis of personality. This is explained in terms of the theory of the Limit and the Infinite, which does not occur outside Western tradition, and so is not present in the Oriental systems which Guénon and Schuon took to be a standard of completeness. In the same context, the Great Chain of Being is shown to include the self in a continuous gradation of being from Highest to lowest, as opposed to the simple dichotomy between pure reality and the realm of *Maya* which Guénon and Schuon took over from Hinduism. Where any dichotomy is an issue, the individual self must still be necessary as the conscious medium in which it could exist, and that guarantees its reality outside that of the dichotomy.

The same principles are applied to the immortality of the soul and conditions of its salvation in Chapter 7. The reasons for the differences between Oriental beliefs and those common to Christianity and Platonism are given. For Oriental thought, there is a real discontinuity between the individual psychic self and its transcendental principle, or 'divine spark'. Such a discontinuity could only be a relationship within the soul to which it was known, failing which, there could be nowhere else in which it could reside. There is therefore no point in ignoring the fact that 'higher' and 'lower' elements in the self presuppose a common substance to which both are relative, except where the self is conceived only as ego.

By a strange irony, the basic disjunction between the higher self or *Atman* and the individual self in Oriental thought is an almost exact parallel of the Cartesian conception of soul and body where neither has anything in common with the other. The fact that contemporary thought does not bother to extend its rejection of Cartesian dualism to other, equally insoluble dualisms shows how little it is able to see through the outward forms of things. An error can be seen if it appears in the work of one philosopher, but not if it appears in a religious tradition. This recalls the problem with the essential reality when one can prove a theorem when the triangle is called ABC, but not when it is called DEF.

This is followed by an account of the Platonic idea of salvation. Since Platonism is so widely heard of, it is extraordinary that hardly anyone in today's world, even among the educated, knows what this is. One would expect to find it in the works of scholars in this field, but it is usually ignored there because of the prevalence of religious unbelief. At the same time, nothing is said about it by theologians, who do not want to express a non-confessional conception which would be hard to argue against and even harder to dissociate oneself from the practice of.

Perhaps strangest of all is the fact that there is never any discussion of this form of salvation in the writings of Guénon and Schuon and their followers. Although they are theoretically committed to an openness to all different traditional forms, they somehow ignore a universal spiritual principle which is undeniably traditional, probably because they do not wish to examine alternatives to a very simple monistic idea of salvation which is really an act of self-verification by the Absolute. How traditional and how orthodox this idea really is can be judged from the fact that it no more requires the grace of faith than does the belief that two twos must forever make four.

In chapter 8 the mystical subject of the union between human beings and God is shown to involve the nature of personhood in ourselves and in God equally. In the light of what has been explained about personality, the word 'union' in this context must mean what it says, and not simply the elimination of one side of the relation. This is supported by reference to the Principle of Plenitude, which also implies the existence of an element in each created being which is continuous by nature with that of God without actually being God. There would thus be a pre-existent principle of contact between human souls and God which can be brought into act.

The way in which these Neoplatonic ideas connect with Christianity is explained so that Christian personalism can be seen to correspond to the idea of substance discussed theoretically in the foregoing. The mediating role of Christ in relation to mankind is shown to correspond to these conceptions, and also, that Christianity comprises something essential to all religions.

In the light of such ideas, many readers may be willing to conclude that Christianity and Platonism are not a choice. However, they should note that this does not mean that either of them could be reduced to the other, which would be to misunderstand them both. Neither should it be taken to mean that Christianity should be equated solely with the exoteric and Platonism solely with the esoteric. Their relations are more complex than that, because they both include elements of both the exoteric and the esoteric. But what is an issue here is the feature of esoteric philosophy which lies in its role of throwing light on what the practice of religion must mean on the plane of pure knowledge. For some, this is a spiritual necessity, without which their faith would be empty and unstable.

The final chapter confronts the specially challenging issue of reconciling the spiritual conceptions of immortality, as in Chapters 7 and 8, with the orthodox belief in the resurrection of the body. To many minds, they belong to such different realms of thought that one can only choose the one or the other. I show that this is not the case by accounting for the physical element in personal salvation, without which it would not be fully personal.

The ideas advanced in this book are all in the deepest sense traditional, and in no way mean a retreat from the esoteric perspective as such. They rather mean a transposition of it to more subtle and universal grounds, thanks to which it can combine with any religion without the least alteration of its doctrine. All that needs to be changed is one's understanding of oneself. This marks a significant difference between it and the esoteric conception of Guénon and Schuon, which was so identified with a doctrine peculiar to one tradition alone that it had to mean the adoption of a heterodox belief for these who belong to the Theistic religions.

This conception also involved a confusion between the esoteric and the exoteric for the further reason that the idea of the self which was used in it was never adequately separated from the ordinary common sense idea of it, where it is equated with the ego. That idea of the self is peculiar to the exoteric, which is why Guénon's and Schuon's ideas mean more an intensification of the exoteric than the true esoteric. But given the principles explained in the following chapters, it is possible to understand these traditionalists on a different basis, while understanding the real identity of the self in the context of its religious values. This does not mean that there is any intention of innovating anything here, but rather to return the esoteric to its Hermetic roots, and the function it had always had in Western spiritual tradition, before the higher wisdom was taken over in the West by an Oriental wisdom which was taken to be superior on account of its freedom from the complexities of the Incarnation. There are some truths which have been in eclipse for too long, and the aim of the following chapters is to release them from their undeserved obscurity.

1

Reflections on the Stone

Therefore thus says the Lord God, Behold I am laying in Zion for a foundation a stone, a tested stone, a precious cornerstone, of a sure foundation: He who believes will not stumble.
Isaiah 28:16

Tradition, Philosophy, and Gnosis

The orthodox interpretation of the above text in Christian tradition is always that the stone represents Christ, the promised Messiah, as is also the case in comparable texts, such as 'the stone which the builders rejected,' in the Psalms. This symbolism of the stone was adopted from more ancient uses, however, and the latter may be the means of connecting it with the so-called Philosophers' Stone, especially as historical revelation will normally correspond to a universal and atemporal order. The idea of the 'stone' naturally evokes the idea of philosophy and its creative endeavours in a traditional context, and we may wonder what place it has there.

For most of those who follow the ideas of Guénon and Schuon, the emphasis in traditionalist thought is overwhelmingly on gnosis, rather than on either philosophy or empirical knowledge, because the modern deviation from tradition is attributable to the reduction of metaphysical truths first to matters of individual speculation, and then finally to the fads of public opinion. There is no doubt that changes of this kind have taken place, and their negative results are only too well known, so that advocacy of more human forms of knowledge may seem to be in conflict with the restoration of tradition.

To some, there may appear to be something absurd about the implicit claim that gnosis is not enough. How should the highest and completest knowledge need to be supplemented? One answer to this can be seen to lie in the very exactitude and finality of gnosis, which link it inseparably to the realm of the finite, a defect which indicates that it needs to be completed by something else, since man was made for the infinite. (This finitude characterizes the mode of being of gnosis, not its theoretical content, of course; these two things should not be confused.) Conversely, while the outreach of philosophical thought lacks the ordered perfection of gnosis, it does answer to man's dynamic relation to the infinite. There should thus be an overall equality between the two, that is, between a precise and complete, but finite, knowledge, and one which is untidy and ever-incomplete, but adapted to the infinite in its operation. The distinction highlighted by this simple dichotomy comprises something which must always be felt as long as mankind is in a temporal state.

These reflections are prompted by what has been written on this subject by Cardinal Joseph Ratzinger in recent years, especially where he says that gnosis alone is the negation of philosophy for the reasons just mentioned, that philosophy is a pursuit of truth where the results are never predictable or final (*The Nature and Mission of Theology*, p28). It thus expresses a conjunction between knowledge and the flowing process of life lived in time, whence it is adequate to the whole human state on its temporal and intellectual levels.

Quite apart from the weight we allow to theoretical comparisons between philosophy and gnosis, there remains the undoubted fact that philosophy was always a part of both Christian and Moslem civilizations throughout the Middle Ages, where it existed alongside both gnosis and religious belief. It had a mediating role between the individual and the universal truths of religion and gnosis, enabling the individual to make the received truths his own in a fully personal manner, without having to be just a receptacle of truths.

In view of its role in the traditions alone, then, we should not have the right to equate philosophy as a whole with the purely individualistic exploration of reality without revelation which it has become today. But if we are to allow that it is ultimately a dimension of the spirit without being gnosis, what would its validity derive from?

There is no doubt that for the traditions it was the expression of a substantial reality, which was called the Philosophers' Stone or the *lapis*, and a good many other things besides, such as the Unique (or One) Thing, the Divine Water, the Lion, and the Sophic Hydrolith. Under this diversity of names it was not distinguished from the *prima materia*, as I shall try to show. Attempts to explain what these terms mean always run the risk of ending up in a quagmire of obscurities which has to some extent been caused deliberately, but the attempt is necessary if we are to clarify the spiritual role of philosophy, that is, its relation to revealed religion in a traditional context.

This subject would become less obscure if it could be shown to be connected with a generally acknowledged reality, albeit one which is usually thought of only in connection with gnosis. Despite the references in scripture like the one under the heading, the *lapis* (understood as the philosophers' stone) is not so much conveyed by revelation as presupposed by it, as the receiver which corresponds by nature to the Divine initiative. It is something more than a creature, but equally it is not God, an idea which is familiar in traditional thought where it is a question of an element in the human soul which transcends creation and relates directly to God. This is frequently to be found in Eckhart, as where he says:

> There is an agent in the soul such that if the soul were wholly this, it would be uncreated, [and furthermore], Without the above-mentioned agent, God acts not at all. Whatever God gives, he gives through it, and if God should give us himself without that agent, we would not accept him, nor would he be to our taste.[1]

It is understood theologically that it is only in the innermost realm of the human spirit that the image of God can be said to reside. This is immovably part of us, so that failure to live in harmony with this divine principle must result in an ultimate inner conflict and self-contradiction. A modern expression of the same idea is given by Philip Sherrard where he says that 'patristic theologians do recognize the presence in man of something which, if it is

1. *Defense,* IX, 3, and 6, Meister Eckhart, R.B. Blakney, tr. (New York: Harper Torchbooks, 1941).

not divine, is yet not undivine; which, if it is not uncreated, is yet not created.'[2]

Sherrard is emphasizing the point that this principle is not just another name for God, as simplistic ways of thinking might take it to be. On the contrary, the peculiar nature of the consequences which follow from it is owing to the fact that it is neither God nor nature, but something sharing the attributes of both, and that human nature can be to varying degrees conformed to it. Nevertheless, most of the things said about it have been outside mainstream theology, if we take alchemical writings into account, and it is from them that we can learn more about the role of this 'divine spark' in the life of the spirit.

The Stone in Tradition

Traditional accounts of the Stone do not always distinguish it from the *prima materia*, as where both are referred to as the *Unica Res* (the unique or only thing) and 'Adam and Microcosm'.[3] This implies that the usage of Hermetic thought differs here from that of Neoplatonism, for which matter is the lowest of realities, a mere empty and unstable receptivity. Instead, it is said to be 'the first *hyle* of the wise, the *prima materia* of the perfect body' and is said to be a substance in which everything is contained in a positive way, by which it has a creative power as an originative principle in nature.[4]

Jung quotes Mylius' statement that it is 'the pure subject and the unity of forms', with both passive and active aspects. We are also told that this mysterious substance is called *radix ipsius* (root of itself), and that 'because it roots in itself it is autonomous and dependent on nothing.'[5] But the supremacy it has in relation to other creatures does not include any question of its creating the world or itself; it has therefore a necessary autonomy in relation to nature, whereas in relation to God, this autonomy is something delegated. There are obviously close analogies between it and both God and the world as

2. *The Rape of Man and Nature* (Ipswich: Golgonooza Press, 1987), chap. 1, p32.
3. C.G. Jung, *Psychology and Alchemy*, III (London: Routledge, 1953), chap. 4, I.
4. Ibid., III, chap. 1, III.
5. Ibid., III, chap. 4, I–II.

a whole, as might be expected of something which is a focal point for so many realities:

> The definition of this spherical being as . . . 'the most serene God', sheds a special light on the perfect 'round' nature of the *lapis* which arises from and constitutes the primal sphere; hence the *prima materia* is often called *lapis*.[6]

At the same time, it is distinguished from God in this text as having arisen, like the world, from a *massa confusa* comprising all the elements. But this does not help us to understand why, in view of its subtlety, 'stone' should have been so prominent among the names used for this subject, when in its religious context it never had a name at all, except where it was referred to as the 'divine spark' in an unofficial manner.

James Hillman's explanation[7] is that this is because, like a physical stone, it has a power to force its presence on our attention by its impenetrable and irreducible quality. Everything in nature from flowing water to roots of trees has to yield to the presence of stones, which combine a certain power with inactivity. They can often punish those who ignore their presence. Stone-like properties, he says, are an emblem of freedom from subjectivity, and not merely as a quantity of hard and enduring material, but as a unique individuality, different from that of every other stone. Thus it evokes the idea of the monad.

The last point shows that it is not too much of a paradox that a very subtle reality could force itself on our attention as a stone does. The essential point here is individuation. Persons or souls encounter one another as quasi-atomic realities, which is why the soul is referred to in philosophy as a 'simple substance'. Just as the physical stone shows the qualities of impenetrability and irreducibility, so the individual soul is impenetrable inasmuch as it is the container of all natural forces in its representation of the world, to which it is not itself external.

6. Ibid., III, chap. 4, III.

7. See 'Concerning the Stone', *Sphinx* 5 (London: The London Convivium for Archetypal Studies, 1993).

Here, then, are some representative observations about the Stone, which must now be linked with what was said above about the quasi-divine principle in the soul, and the resulting implications for philosophy. If this 'naturally supernatural' principle, as Schuon would call it, were considered, not in relation to God, but as a normative principle for both man and nature, much that has been said of the *lapis* would be relevant to it. Contradictory attributes like those of 'stone' and 'water' would not be surprising in something which was an archetype and an epitome of the complex range of realities which make up the natural order. On the one hand, a deepening understanding of this interior reflection of the divine must be implicitly redemptive, as historically it was taken to be, while on the other, the redemption and regeneration brought by revealed religion must *inter alia* bring the individual into a closer communion with this same interior reality. These two movements of the soul, far from being exclusive, have always been conceived as working together in the same persons, at least when understood in a context of Hermeticism.

The Lapis and the Monad

This brings us to a significant double meaning in this interior agency: because the *lapis* mediates between God and creation, it can be seen with equal reason as either the base of a mystical or gnostic *ascensus* to God, or as the apex of an integrating movement in the natural order. Such a conception would suffice to connect the mysterious, protean Stone with a basic idea which is accepted in most forms of traditional wisdom. The duality involved in this idea is no more than what is implied in the duality of the human state, consisting as it does of body and soul, and residing on the boundary of nature and the supernatural. On this basis, I shall try to account for some consequences which would naturally be realized by the creative work of philosophy.

While the *lapis* is unique in itself, it exists in as many instances as there are persons, so that something qualitatively equivalent to the Whole exists in every being which forms part of the Whole, giving a special meaning to the idea that 'all is one'. In this case, the Whole would in some sense be present in every part of the All, an idea which Leibniz expresses in the *Monadology* where he says that souls are

> living mirrors or images of the universe of created things, but those minds are also images of the Deity or Author of nature Himself, capable of knowing the system of the universe . . . each mind being like a small divinity in its own sphere.[8]

This matches the idea that 'the *sulphur philosophorum* is one substance in which everything is contained.'[9]

Such an interpenetrating view of the one and the many has always found a place in Christian cultures, because the doctrine of the Eucharist follows a similar pattern. Each consecrated Host becomes the Body of the Lord, and at the same time, so does each particle of each Host; the unique One is infinitely multiplied, and not merely as a symbol. At the same time, the Incarnation and the Ascension reflect the relation between the divine and the human which is a model for each human life inasmuch as it is true to its destiny. Leibniz' philosophy is deeply influenced by the Hermetic tradition, which is distinguished as a meeting place of philosophy and magic, with its idea of a reality which is microcosmic through and through. Parts not only reflect the whole, but have powers of attraction and influence among themselves in proportion to the similarities between the ways in which they reflect the world and the degrees to which they do so. From thence come the evocative powers of magic and the influences of astrology:

> Each portion of matter may be conceived as a garden full of plants, and as a pond full of fish. But every branch of each plant, every member of each animal, and every drop of their liquid parts is itself likewise a similar garden or pond.[10]

This power of reflecting the whole of things has also implications which are relevant to the idea of the *lapis*, because the soul, in

8. Leibniz, *The Monadology and Other Philosophical Writings*, Robert Latta, tr., (Oxford: OUP, 1993), 83 (hereafter cited as *Monadology*).

9. Jung, ibid., III, chap. I, III.

10. *Monadology*, 67.

reflecting in its own mode the nature of an indestructible universe will itself be indestructible in the same way, a way which belongs among the stone-like properties. Similarly, this goes with a certain impenetrability, which results simply from the fact that it is in a real sense a whole and not a part, and so cannot be directly subject to external natural agencies in the way that the ego and the contents of sense perception are. By definition, then, souls or monads can be subject only to God in a direct sense, while their interactions could only take place by the indirect way of interior changes which create new sets of relations or weaken or strengthen existing relations among them.

Such properties as the above are the context in which philosophy becomes a condition for the realization of the human state as such, not least because the subject of philosophy is reality as a whole, while a representation of the world as a whole is part of the essence of each rational being. Such is a primary aspect of the spiritual soul, as compared with the souls of animals, which relate only to parts of the world and so are necessarily peripheral to the human state. A microcosmic being must philosophize (judge reality as a whole) in order to be itself, therefore. This has consequences for religion because the perspective of faith also places man in relation to reality as a whole just as much as to God. Both faith and philosophy involve a positive and conscious relation to the infinite.

Implications for the Esoteric

The above consequences apply in particular to a feature which both exoteric and esoteric religion, as usually understood today, rather strangely have in common. However much they differ in other ways, they both see the individual person as a negation, or as a blank to be filled in, so to speak. Thus both are equally dominated by the point of view from which God is everything and man is nothing, even though there are doubts as to how literally this is meant. In exoteric religion this point of view arises because of the need to give first place to the personal relation between God and the individual, which is taken simply as a relation between the infinite and the finite. This is balanced, but only in an *ad hoc* manner, by the understanding that this relationship is of importance to God. It is therefore very strange that most contemporary forms of esoteric religion should espouse the same view of God and man as in the above, since, for them, simplified conceptions are neither necessary nor appropriate.

Part of the reason for this is that in today's world, both exoteric and esoteric religion are dominated by the same naive common sense assumptions about the self. These are (1) that the person is his ego and nothing else, and (2) that the next higher alternative to the ego must be God. In this regard the exoteric and the esoteric differ only on the point that for the exoteric the distinction between God and ego is final, whereas for the esoteric it can be dissolved from the position of the ego. This kind of self-transcendence is made necessary only by the limitations of the common sense idea of the self-as-ego, and not by the real nature of the self as soul, which will be explained later.[11]

In a complete esoteric philosophy, where man's relation to God is seen in a context of impersonal realities which transcend the usual limitations of understanding, the spiritual meaning of the individual should be explicable with a new depth and clarity, not despaired of as an illusion. That this is so often not the case indicates that even some of the most intelligent exponents of the esoteric remain subject to the mindset of modern times which does not see the meaning of the microcosm in relation to God. Thus they still think instinctively in terms of a relation between something huge and something tiny, as though that was all there was to it.

The objection to this from a Hermetic point of view is that it springs from a quantitative way of looking at the world, which is usually an unconscious side-effect of modern science, which is not concerned with the qualitative infinity in beings who are only parts in an external way. The more we get away from a mistaken use of quantitative thought, the more we shall be free from defeatist views about the value of the individual as such. The reality which transcends the person is still a function of the person, because he has a mode of equivalence to the Whole. This makes it much easier to understand the truth that the things which individuals intend, do,

11. See chap. 2, *Dualism and the Soul.*

and refrain from doing, have an effect on the world which goes far beyond anything they are able to perceive.

Only like can truly act on like, and in this case it is the rational being who is in a real sense equivalent to a world, and who can therefore act significantly on the world of which his ego is outwardly a part. Conversely, the actions of animals have no such independent power over nature because they are solely parts in relation to the Whole, having no share in man's central place in nature. There are both spiritual and magical implications for this kind of relation which mankind has to its world, connected with the idea that there is a point at which religion, philosophy, psychology and magic have a region in common.

The reality of some such convergence as this was believed in by Jung, and it was the basis of his idea of the necessary role of the individual, to which he opposed collectivistic beliefs. He regarded the latter as irrational, because denials of human individuality are necessarily denials of the creative principle which is fundamental to all value-systems, besides which, they deny the possibility of redemption on a personal basis.

Consequently, all systems which downgrade the individual are ultimately self-defeating; neither collective entities nor mystical systems can of themselves supply the consciousness necessary to make them work. Equally, the higher forms of knowledge can have no direct power over individual consciousness, but only what the latter can see it right to employ. To some, this may appear only too obvious, but there are many who are so blinded by the external and quantitative aspect of things that they hardly see it at all, or regard it as a delusion.

A Meaning for Autonomy

What has been said about the basis of individuality can be linked to the question of whether the person or monad can be said to have autonomy. This issue can be seen in the fact that two pillars of received wisdom are that man must be open and receptive to whatever Providence may send or allow, and that he is responsible for the control of his own thoughts. It seems that there is a flat contradiction between these two precepts, at least as long as openness is misunderstood as a degree of passivity which would be untrue to our essential nature.

In reality, the reception of things and selection among them are separable only for thought, not in actual practice. These two processes correspond to the autonomy of the *radix ipsius* and to the fact that it did not create itself, and so must always accept an aspect of relativity for itself. Here again, it is for philosophy to mediate between the absolute and the relative where they are manifest in our own constitution.

While every mind is active in selecting its objects, and passive in the reception of them, there are many differences possible in the proportions between the two. The more the active power of selection is developed, the greater the degree of free will, since the degree of freedom of the will is in practice dependent on the size of the sphere in which it operates, even though in principle it is present in everyone. The complexities of this function can be seen from the fact that not only are there many degrees of this selective activity, there are at the same time innumerable criteria by which it can operate.

The process of selection is thus a form of 'self-expression' in a quite exact sense of the word. The least effective form of it follows the broadest of all criteria, that of pleasure, but without trying to judge the reasons why it is pleasurable or to compare different kinds of pleasure. Whatever its degree or quality, this expression of autonomy is not just a matter of culture, but is a characteristic of mind as such, in the light of the foregoing. It is reflected only partially by the senses, because on the one hand they automatically continue to convey to us the same things as long as we are present to them, regardless of our choice; in this respect they are passive, while on the other hand choice must require either the substitution of other objects or the transfer of one's physical presence.

As the mind makes its selections among the contents of its world, these choices of object not only express and reinforce the quality it already has, but they also have a determining influence on the objects which will come to it, as it were *ab extra*, at future times. While there is a clear common sense distinction between things we choose to perceive and think about, and things which come to us unbidden and without warning, this is only because the latter seem not to be chosen, but nevertheless they are chosen in the same sense as we choose the experiences comprised in a journey simply by our initial decision to travel from A to B. In a more subtle way, the things that engage the mind and will at a given time will place one in the 'qualitative locality' of those things, so that others coherent with them will later be encountered, apparently by accident. The more purposive our selection of mental objects or stimuli, the more clearly this effect on future experience will be felt, while in proportion as we fall short in this respect, the more future events will assume a random character.

The contents of the world appear in the mind as so many different determinations of it, rather as clay is made into innumerable pieces of pottery. The mind is in effect an infinite substance which receives an infinity of modifications ranging from basic sensations to the subtlest kinds of insight. If it should still appear that the autonomy attributed to it is contradicted by experience, the relation of the mind to its world must be seen in the light of the different possibilities offered by the power of control. The chances and mischances of individual lives are full of examples of apparently uncontrolled happenings which are in reality under exactly as much control as are orderly and constructive ones, only with the difference that in the former it is an ignorant and foolish use of control.

So with the human mind and its relation to life in the world: even its worst failures never amount to a loss of its directing role, but prove only the flaws in its direction. This intrinsic autonomy of the self in relation to its world finds a typical expression in philosophy, and this does not imply any conflict with the authority of religion, because orthodox religious teachings, if lived out, lead to a state of freedom in relation to nature which corresponds precisely to philosophy's theoretical transcendence.

The Relation to Grace

The traditional role of philosophy, based on the above properties of consciousness, has implications which are not consistent with the majority views of tradition today, because it cannot coincide with that of gnosis. The necessity of this role of individual selection and creative action would imply that a spiritual realization which was solely universal and non-personal, as is maintained by Ananda Coomaraswamy,[12] for example, would be no more of an ideal than one which was solely individual. In reality, individuality can have spiritual potentialities just as much as the profane ones it is usually associated with, while conversely there is nothing to prevent anti-individualistic systems from serving profane delusions as well as wisdom, as modern history shows.

Finally, what has been said in regard to the potentialities of the individual has been said from a specifically human point of view, that is, without its being directly related to God, who alone can act on the human will. But the fact that man is nevertheless dependent on grace to make positive choices has not been referred to, only because the factor of Divine causality does not detract anything from the reality of an independent principle in mankind, nor from the fact that every tendency to realize it increases the natural autonomy of the person. Without this, there would be nothing for Divine causality to act on in any case. Neither does it call for any modification to the idea that each soul or monad is as it were the theatre of its spiritual progress.

There is a point at which man's control coincides with that of God, as might be expected from the nature of the *lapis*, inasmuch as it is said to be 'the water from which everything originates, in which errors are made and in which the error itself is corrected.'[13] These things imply that man's role as mediator between God and the world is an essential part of the plan of creation, so that all attempts fully to realize this possibility will necessarily be a cooperation with the will of God.

12. See 'The Pertinence of Philosophy', *Sacred Web 1*.
13. C.G. Jung, *Psychology and Alchemy*, III, chap. III.

2

Dualism and the Soul

Introductory Note for Traditionalists

It may seem that this account of Dualism is out of place here, because for most followers of neo-traditionalism, traditional wisdom is now thought to be closely allied to monistic mysticism. Those who argue for alternatives to this will be told that they are disputing about a kind of wisdom which has been taught by persons of the highest intelligence and virtue, whom we cannot emulate, let alone surpass. But however true this may be, it is also true that the same observations apply to even greater numbers of those who have taught according to dualistic principles. On this point I part ways with Guénon and Schuon. Their implied belief that such traditional masters as Ramanuja, al-Ghazzali, Maimonides, and St Thomas Aquinas were all incapable of teaching Monism because they lacked the necessary intelligence, knowledge, or sanctity, may be acceptable to some, but to others it seems self-refuting. For the latter, tradition presents us with too wide a range of realities for it to be identifiable with any one metaphysical system. The alternative considered here does not have to be an attempt to claim absoluteness for something which could only be relative, since duality, the archetype of all relativities, cannot itself be one more relativity, which I hope will appear from what follows. Arguably, the duality of soul and God could be an ultimate reality, if it could be shown that mystical self-transcendence was explicable as an internal development in the soul, prompted by its relation to God.

Dualism and the Soul

Modern Anti-Dualism

Dualistic thought is out of favour today because it is widely felt to have been tried and found wanting, and not only by philosophers, but this may be because the objections to it are taken for granted, rather than thought through. A re-examination of the arguments for Dualism is now overdue, because it seems to most minds today that the only realistic alternatives to it are those of materialism or monistic pantheism. If, however, the metaphysical basis of Christianity and the other Monotheistic religions is in fact Dualism, we could not expect them to sustain themselves in the face of criticism, if their theoretical basis was rejected. Much of the opposition to dualistic philosophy comes from the psychological fact that the leading thinkers in both modern science and monistic mysticism are equally unable to see that their chosen realities cannot really be independent of the consciousness of the individual. There are in fact profound reasons for the duality of God in relation to the soul, which are only ignored because of the prevailing habits of thought.

A further reason for this kind of study is to be found in the light Dualism can throw on the nature of the soul and personal identity. More generally still, this form of thought answers to so many realities that alternative explanations can appear forced. To make this clearer, we need to take a look at the present state of the thought opposed to it, and then examine in turn its cosmic relevance, some of the standard arguments for it, and finally its implications for morality, culture, and religion. Dualistic thought is centered on a duality of soul and body which is now unjustly identified with Descartes' philosophy. This is unfortunate for Dualism, because Descartes adapted this traditional idea in a way which equated the soul with its thought, and made the distinction between it and the body too extreme for their interaction to be understood. The philosophy of the twentieth century has been dominated by a reaction against Descartes, which has been widely taken to be a reaction against Dualism in general, so that it has ended by becoming almost a term of abuse, after having been taken for a reality since very early times.

The first question to be considered is: How far is this reaction justified? Indications that it may not be justified appear, for example, in the way that materialistic and monistic thought enjoy a willing suspension of disbelief that is not afforded to other philosophies; this would imply motives more social and political than philosophical. There is a tacit conviction that the truth must be *simple,* despite the fact that this belief is not supported either by logical reasoning or by experience. Where this is expressed in anti-Cartesianism, a certain irrationality also appears in the fact that when we attribute the influence of Dualism to Descartes, we are implicitly attributing to him the power of imposing his own peculiar way of thinking on a whole civilization for three centuries together. In reality, this kind of power is so rare that it is usually considered an attribute of the founders of religions, not of philosophers.

Conversely, a more rational line of criticism would suggest that what Descartes really did was to identify a certain element in the way in which human minds have always worked, and create a system around it. Being founded on a universal tendency of the human mind, it would then be sure of acceptance for perfectly natural reasons. This explanation, however, would take away our right to reproach Descartes with the problems raised by Dualism as such. The fault, if fault it was, would have to be with us all. That, however, would be more rational than to attribute supernatural powers to a secular thinker who is believed to be discredited.

Because of a widespread desire for unification and thereby simplification, anti-dualist philosophies have become so prevalent that anyone could be forgiven for thinking these philosophies have proved their point and are able to provide a complete and satisfactory account of reality. But this is only an appearance. It has been pointed out by one modern philosopher, Geoffrey Madell,[1] that all attempts to create a working philosophy which would unite everything on the physical level have failed for one reason or another, partly because thought possesses properties such as Intentionality[2]

1. See his *Mind and Materialism* (Edinburgh: Edinburgh Univ. Press, 1988).

2. *Intentionality* applies to the way in which things in the physical world owe their properties to our thoughts and practical purposes. I say that a chunk of glass with a hollow in the middle is an *ash tray* because of my own tendency to use it for

and Indexicality,[3] which seem to be impervious to this kind of treatment.

In the same context, another contemporary philosopher, John Searle, refers to the fact that the denial of Dualism means in practice a denial of consciousness itself, and that modern philosophers who argue for this are arguing for something which not only most people do not believe, but which they themselves do not believe except, perhaps, in the lecture-room. As he puts it: 'We ought to stop saying things that are obviously false,' although Searle himself is not a dualist. In theory, we could also eliminate Dualism from the opposite direction, so to speak, by retaining consciousness and denying the existence of the outside world instead, but that course would meet with a more concerted rejection than the former option, but only for human reasons, not logical ones. Nevertheless, some such position is in fact adopted by post-modernism, where it tries to make the use of language independent of any external referents.

According to Searle's criticism, the denial of consciousness is not sustainable because consciousness cannot be reduced to an appearance of some other phenomenon. It is a special case in which the appearance is the reality. It is thus the container and basis of phenomena as such. In this respect it is quite unlike, say, the sensation of heat, or the vibrations of atoms and molecules. The latter are two typical phenomena within consciousness, and so in principle

that purpose. Similarly, one collection of people is a party, while another is an auction, but what makes these things what they are is the intentionality of those who go to them, that is, the thought in each mind 'this is going to be a party' or 'this is going to be an auction.' Without this, the efforts to organize such things would be in vain. Yet in every such case, the only *physical* reality is just a collection of human beings. A 'theory of everything,' as scientists understand it, would therefore not be able to make sense of either Indexicality or Intentionality.

3. *Indexicality* is a property of things by which they have unique reference to one another, and it appears where statements are said to be 'about' something. For example, we may have a scientifically complete description of all the people in a room, without its being able to include such facts as that 'this person is me,' and 'that one is you,' or that the universe contains an individual such as me and one such as you. Thus indexicality relates to a class of beings none of which can be substituted for others, whereas for science, all entities in a given class are open to substitution.

reducible one to the other, as in fact science has shown them to be. Consciousness, on the other hand could only be reduced to something else if that something else was really outside it. This would require us to be conscious of something which consciousness never reached, which would be simply a contradiction. For reasons such as these, a successful non-dualist philosophy remains to this day only an aspiration.

In the light of the current situation, then, there need be no fear that a re-examination of Dualism must mean denying an inevitable progress, or disputing anything which was certainly established. One problem with the denial of consciousness is that we must retain all the objects which were taken to be objects of consciousness and explain them in a new way which would be more convincing than that of Dualism. Materialistic thought is tied to the assumption that the world and its contents are independent of our knowledge of them, not merely in their essence and origin, but also in the very forms we believe them to have. Such a view of reality is least of all able to confront the question of appearance and reality, since it takes no account of the contribution which our minds make to the outside world as we know it.

From a dualistic point of view, this would amount to an attempt to retain an effect without its cause or an attribute without its substance, as if the Cheshire cat's grin really could remain when the cat was gone. I shall try to show later that the form which objective realities have for us owes its character to the way in which consciousness grasps it, which would rule out the 'givenness' of external reality as required by materialism. Not that the world is created by consciousness, but that much of what makes it recognizable for us is so created. The relationship between consciousness and the objects in the outside world, I shall suggest, may be compared with that between the water in a pond and the ripples on its surface. Thus for all their independence of origin, the objects of consciousness would only be known to us *qua* modifications of that consciousness.

History and Cosmic Conditions

Turning now to the historical background of Dualism, it can be seen that from the earliest times it appeared in cosmological thought, where it had a significance which overflowed the boundaries of the spiritual and the physical. It entered into religion as a belief in opposing gods of light and darkness, like that of Ormuzd and Ahriman in Persian religion, while the duality of body and soul has also been a part of religious thought from very early times, both in Judaism and Christianity, and in other traditions, like that of Egypt. There is a variety of biblical texts referring to this subject, two clear examples of which are: 'Look upon all the works of the Most High; they likewise are in pairs, one the opposite of the other.' (Sirach 33:15), and: 'And fear not them who only kill the body but cannot kill the soul' (Matt. 10:28).

The duality of soul and body was developed by Plato and Aristotle, through whose thought and its offshoots it has remained current up to modern times, which implies that there must be at least something perennially meaningful about it, whatever problems it may give rise to. Plato and Aristotle were building on an existing tradition for which the dualities, oppositions, and complementarisms in nature were one of the earliest incentives to speculation. The Pythagorean cosmology interpreted nature in terms of ten pairs of opposites (ten itself being a significant number), as follows: limit and unlimited; odd and even; unity and plurality; right and left; male and female; rest and motion; straight and crooked; light and darkness; good and evil; square and oblong.

The changes and interactions between these opposites were thought to make up the cosmic process, although there is hardly any limit to the number of other such pairings which seem to enter into the essence of things, e.g., subject and object; form and matter; body and soul; freedom and necessity; cause and effect; self and ego; quality and quantity; active and passive; substance and accident; positive and negative; heaven and earth; heaven and hell; eternity and time; life and death; love and hate; nature and nurture; matter and energy.

The fact that the human mind naturally thinks in terms of things in opposing pairs, either member of which evokes the other, is always liable to prompt the question as to whether these dualities are, as such, part of the natural order which we perceive, or whether they result only from the way in which the human mind selects its objects. In answer to this question, we could do worse than refer to the dual way in which the brain is constructed. Our brains consist of two main distinct parts, these being the cerebrum, the larger part in the upper and front position, and the cerebellum, the smaller part in the lower rear position. These two parts of the brain are both divided into right-hand and left-hand hemispheres, which serve very different purposes, as is now well known. The left side of the cerebrum is used for logical and verbal activities, while the right side is for imaginative and intuitive thought.

In regard to the body, the *right-hand* side of the cerebrum interacts with the *left-hand* side of the body, both in regard to sensation and in initiating movement. Likewise, its left hemisphere interacts with the right-hand side of the body. In contrast to this, the left and right sides of the cerebellum interact with the same sides of the body as their own. This means that the left hemisphere of the cerebellum has to communicate with the right hemisphere of the cerebrum, and vice-versa, wherever there is an experience on either side of the body which involves both parts of the brain; while the right hemisphere of the cerebellum must communicate with the left hemisphere of the cerebrum.

These facts about the brain make it look well suited to the role of a duality-generator in a way which apparently supports the notion that the dualities we see in the world reveal more about ourselves than about the world. However, the formation of the brain took place long before human consciousness had any part to play. It took shape under cosmic conditions which had the power to determine the form of the brain in accordance with their own nature. Whether the brain emerged from the natural order by evolution, or whether it was created by God so as to be able to understand and reflect the nature of the universe, the implication is the same: the structure of the brain reflects an objective reality, so that any dualistic tendencies that this gives rise to need not mean a projection upon the world of anything alien to it.

If we now look into the workings of nature to find a physical source for the processes which have led to our physical dualities, there is a huge range of relevant phenomena to be considered. To begin with the inner structure of matter, the atom of each chemical element has principal parts which are equal numbers of positively-charged protons and negatively-charged electrons, since all the elements start with the hydrogen atom, which consists of one proton and one electron. Each successive element, as one ascends the periodic table, requires the addition of one more electron and one more proton. Every element therefore comprises a group of pairings between positive and negative sub-atomic particles. The reactions between the elements which form their innumerable compounds are caused by the forces of attraction between the electro-positive and the electro-negative elements, so that their combinations depend on a duality as much as does their inner structure. In the realm of mechanics, the stability of the universe depends on a balance between two classes of force, namely the centrifugal and the centripetal. If either of these were to overcome the other, the universe would either collapse or dissolve, and analogous remarks apply to the rate at which the universe is expanding.

Similarly in the living world, it is easy to see that life depends on a balance between the vegetable and animal kingdoms, because of their opposite uses of oxygen and carbon dioxide. Most species reproduce sexually, so that each new individual must result from two progenitors, and not one, and so create maximum variety. Given this universal role of duality in the matter and energy of the universe, Dualism would appear to be an intellectual image of the cosmic order.

This point brings up the question as to how closely integrated must mind and body be thought to be? If their relation was a very close one, our underlying physical dualities could be expected to have an effect on the direction of our thinking. In this case, thought would most likely have an objectively-based dualistic tendency. Conversely, if there were as little connection between mind and body as Descartes seems to think, the form and tendency of thought need not be affected by its cosmic setting. In this case, it may seem that Dualism need be no more than a possible option, but only seemingly. A disjunction between mind and body which was extreme enough to release the mind from nature in this way would be a truly fundamental instance of duality. Whether mind and body are closely integrated or not, therefore, Dualism should be equally an issue.

Arguments for Dualism in Knowledge

Turning now to the philosophical arguments, for which I shall make use of what has been said on this subject by Arthur Lovejoy,[4] it should be noted first that the truth of duality does not depend on its having to be absolute. That would in fact be contradictory, since every supposedly absolute dualism is always a relationship within a single system. On the contrary, it requires only that the dual realities be comparably real in relation to the principle which transcends their division. Otherwise, if only the transcending unity were real, as Monists think, this unity alone would be as little able to account for the coherent complexity of the real as the opposite idea that only plurality was real.

Of all the instances of duality, the ones most commonly thought of are those of subject and object, and mind and matter. As far as common sense is concerned, this distinction remains meaningful, though it is denied by much of modern philosophy. The problems encountered by this philosophy in eliminating mind and consciousness as a reality distinct from the natural order, are suitable grounds for looking again at the reasons why Dualism was taken to be true in the first place.

The premise that there is a real world, and that it is accessible to both thought and sensation is still compatible with the idea that much of it is owing to the nature of our minds. The world is too real to be only a product of our thoughts, while at the same time our perceptions of the world are far from giving us the whole truth about it. In other words, it can be shown that the perceived world is in many ways not the same as the known world. When we carelessly

4. See his *The Revolt Against Dualism* (London: George Allen and Unwin Ltd., 1930).

say we know something because we have seen or heard it, we are ignoring the fact that much more than sensation had to be involved in this. Recollection, logical deduction, and generalization always have to be applied. This can be seen from the fact that no one could master the content of a book merely by perception of its pages, however much they may stare at them.

In short, we are aware of a certain discontinuity between ourselves and the outside world which the combined action of sensation and our mental faculties can bridge, but without eliminating it. Some aspects of this gap between the material world and our consciousness leave traces which are even physically measurable. Sight and hearing depend on the motion of light and sound waves, both of which travel to us at finite speeds. This opens a gap between our perception of an object and the object in itself. Light from the Moon takes one-and-a-quarter seconds to reach us, and light from the Sun about eight minutes. Light from the stars may take years, which means we could be looking at objects which have ceased to exist since the light we can see left them. But even the tiniest lapse of time between a perception and the source of the perception is enough to show that we are not dealing with the things in themselves. Thus we should not in theory have the right to equate the source of a perception with our sensation of it.

Much of what we know and think about concerns things in the past and future. These things are certainly not directly present, but our ability to think about them is not affected by that. We work with mental representations of things so naturally that we usually do not stop to consider that that is in fact what they are. But in the present moment, things must be different, one would think, because in the present there must be a direct connection between our experience and the things experienced, even if they are distanced by the time intervals between their appearances and our awareness of them. However, it is not hard to show that the contents even of the present moment consist to a large extent of recollections of the immediate past and anticipations of the immediate future.

Besides, even if we had a purely present experience, it would be by no means as objective as we usually imagine. This appears in the perspective distortion which affects nearly everything we see.

Straight railway tracks and the top and bottom edges of walls are seen to converge at their farther ends, even though we know that the objects in question do no such thing. Square and rectangular objects, unless seen centrally from above, are seen as rhombuses or parallelograms. Likewise, circular objects are most often seen as ellipses, and here again, seeing is not believing. We forget this because the distorted figures are mentally translated into rectangles and circles so automatically that this invites comparison with the way in which the upside-down images on our retinas are turned the right way up by the brain.

When we move our observation around stationary solid objects, they are seen to change shape, without anyone believing that that is actually happening. Similarly, objects are seen to grow larger as we approach them and grow smaller as we move away from them, which again we disbelieve because mental judgement is substituted for sense. Common sense assures us that our perceptions of things growing larger and smaller is owing to the fact that a pair of light rays from the top and bottom of an object diverge at a wide angle when the eye is close to them, and at only a small angle when it is distant. But the weakness of this well-known geometrical story is that it presupposes the existence of an object of fixed size for the light rays to make different angles with. The existence of things of constant size was what we wanted to prove, whereas this argument needs the conclusion before it can start. For this reason, then, objects of constant size are not a matter of sensory experience. In all these matters, thought over-rules perception, because hardly anyone doubts that the real world is different from what our senses are telling us.

Another essential way in which the world we perceive differs from the world we believe to be the real one appears in the continuity with which things are believed to exist. For our senses, all the persons, places and things known to us are continually appearing and disappearing without any necessary rule or regularity, except where we impose a rule on them and on ourselves. No matter how often things appear and disappear for sense perception, we take it for granted that they really exist just as continuously as we do ourselves. Here again our conviction results from a mental judgement on our sense-data, because sense perception confirms only our own continuous existence, while that of all other persons and things is just an inference.

The common sense reason why we do not perceive things really passing into and out of existence is, like the previous example, one of question-begging. It argues that we only see things appear and vanish again because we are transferring our attention and activities from one thing to another, and that our ability to divide our attention is always limited. However, if things were really alternately coming into existence and passing out of it, our attention would be transferred perforce, in any case. This situation is quite literally the case with the images we watch in films and on television. The deception of the eye by films leads us to a similar result as in real life, that is, to our conviction that the objects we perceive exist continuously, and that sense is only giving us fluctuating representations of things which are constant in themselves.

This is far from accounting for all the ways in which the perceived world differs from the real world. We also believe that everything in the real world is governed by the natural laws which are investigated by science, despite the fact that none of our normal perceptions presents us with anything of this kind. At first sight, this may seem too sweeping, because laws can be seen in simple instances, as where water extinguishes fire, heat melts solid things, and propulsive force causes motion. But natural non-scientific observation just as often shows these things failing to happen, because the quantities of water, heat, or propulsive force still must be sufficiently great to reveal the laws concerned. This is why such results do not appear with the clarity of laws unless one systematically works out all the applicable possibilities.

When we pass from the sense world to that of the imagination, moreover, even where the objects it forms have the same properties as those of sensorily-perceived ones, natural laws disappear completely. If this realm were part of the natural order, therefore, natural laws would not be laws at all; but if it were not, all experience would be subject to a basic duality. Thus only direct sense experience will sustain natural laws, and not even that, where it is not manipulated.

These examples illustrate the fact that the observation of natural laws is possible only when we set aside all personal motives and interests and subject our activity to the limitations of one particular phenomenon. This is what scientists have to do, of course, and their work thereby consists in excluding relatively inessential things so as to reach the essential ones. That is how many scientists would put it, I think, but the implication is that most human motivations and activities are somehow not fully real, which really shows that the world of science is necessarily an abstraction in relation to natural experience.

But if the world of ordinary experience is not seen to be governed by the laws of nature, this does not mean that it has no law at all. In fact it is very much subject to a law, this being that of one's own will. The will determines what is selected for attention, and for what purposes, and for how long, and its purposes seldom include following through the pattern of a natural law. The will is driven by ends to be achieved as much as by causes in the past, although this teleological property is allowed no place in nature as it is known to science. For this reason again, the world of science can never coincide with the whole of reality; its world always has to be reached by a subtractive process which eliminates purpose, among other things. The fact that the world of science cannot coincide with that of experience is an outstanding example of the breach between what our senses tell us and what we believe actually exists.

Part of the function of sense-perception is to draw a mass of separate things together into a single location, as may be depicted by rays of light meeting at a focal point. In this way, the unrelatedness, separation and mutual exclusion of objects is overcome, and they are transferred to a state where each of them enters into contact with all the others. Here again, we have a way in which the perceived world differs from the objective world: in the physical world, all things are in fact in mutual separation and exclusion, but *qua* perceived, they are all in a state of intercommunication. This form of transcendence is no more than what consciousness requires, and representation is what makes it possible. This has consequences for the form in which the world appears to us. All its scattered contents appear as a structured system with one's own ego at the center, with the contents arranged as it were in concentric shells around this center.

This appearance of the world as always revolving around one's own ego is in fact the price demanded for the ability to take it into consciousness at all. The fact that no one believes that the objective world really revolves round the person who perceives it opens a specially sharp distinction between objective reality and that of representation or appearance. It is impossible to imagine what one's familiar surroundings would look like if they were not all referred to a single center of perception, and this shows how much the form of the perceived world is shaped by the consciousness which receives it.

Some of the above arguments for Dualism are readily understandable by artists, because artistic skill calls for a keen sense of the difference between what is presented by the senses and what we just think is there. Thus a new conception of what is objectively-there depends on an initial separation of the subjective and objective components of perception. The sciences are also concerned with this distinction between appearance and reality in their own way, because the purpose of scientific investigation is to explore the difference between them. It could be said that science is a vastly extended expression of the human mind's way of processing the disorders of perception into objects of constant size and shape and having continuous being. Like art, it both presupposes the distinction between appearance and reality, and works to bridge the gap between them. Dualistic concepts show that this world is not as objective as we like to think it is, but they also mean that we have a power of living outside ourselves, so to speak. As one Dualist philosopher put it, it enables us to go abroad while staying at home. All that is 'out there' is at the same time 'in here'.

Dualism and the Soul

Here, then, are some of the basic arguments for the dualistic theory of knowledge, and it now remains to look at their relevance for the idea of the soul, which I will discuss in the traditional way as the non-material and governing principle which is the counterpart of the body. So far, I have tried to show that the dualist arguments undermine the common sense idea that the world we perceive is a ready-made and self-sustaining reality, by showing how it is distorted and mutilated in the process of being perceived, while at the same time a rectifying process resolves it into what we intuitively believe it must be.

These two processes, without which there could be no question of knowing an outside world, cannot be conceived as being parts of that outside world. They are much more readily understood as manifestations of an immaterial activity at the center of everything, this being the typical activity attributable to the soul. Thus the argument goes that representation commits us to the idea of a Representer, and this is what is normally identified with the soul.

There is, however, a prospect of circularity in this argument which needs clarification. In arguments for the idea of the world as a personal representation, it is more than likely that the agency of the soul is being assumed, even though the necessity for an agent is not proven.[5] How far, therefore, and in what way, can the evidence for representation provide an *independent* support for belief in the soul? It can still be a basis of argument if we admit the possibility of the soul as a working hypothesis from the start, and then examine the way in which the world appears in perception. If this leads to conclusions which account for realities which material things alone do not explain, and a non-material counterpart to the body is appropriate for this, the hypothesis can then be taken to be verified in much the same way as science verifies *its* hypotheses. The idea of representation rests on the fact that the real world is not as it appears strictly to our senses, and this fact is an objective datum as much as any object of sense. In this case, experience is produced out of the objective world by an agency in the self, and is never ready-made.

The reality of the soul as the true core of our being makes a vital difference to the idea of personal identity, that is, how we answer the question 'What am I?' From what can be said about the soul's role in perception, it can be seen that there is one way in which soul and body are not only complementary realities, but that each is exactly the inverse of the other. For the common sense idea of identity—based on the body—the 'I' or self is one more physical entity among

5. See chap. 7, pp 138–139.

others, and it is wholly contained by a physical world which is made up of other such things. It is a certain kind of organism which runs about on the surface of a certain kind of planet, and is therefore relative by definition.

Conversely, for the soul, the body and the whole physical world which the body belongs to, appear as *content*. While the body is essentially something *contained*, the soul is essentially a *container* of phenomena. Its content is a world-representation which has the body or ego at the center. This does not mean that the common sense idea of the self as a physical entity is false in itself, only that it is extremely one-sided. The complete 'I' or self is indeed this physical entity *plus* the world-containing and world-representing soul. The world, as it appears from one's own unique point of view, is in a real sense a part of one's identity as well, therefore.

People are aware that Gilbert Ryle applied the dismissive expression 'the ghost in the machine' to the idea of mind or soul as a substantive reality, but we can now see the irrelevance of this remark once the soul is understood as the container of the representations which make up for us the body and its relations with other physical things. An alleged soul which could be contained by the body, therefore, like an internal organ or an actual ghost in a house, would, on this basis, be just a contradiction. By reason of the soul, therefore, the true and complete self cannot be a passive item in the flow of natural phenomena. A vital part of its being is in effect the *stage* upon which this flow of phenomena is represented and privately made known, in a way which is distinctive to the person concerned.

The full development of personal identity, which includes the activity of soul, points towards the traditional idea of the self as a microcosm. The idea of the microcosm is that of an epitome of all realities, from the most subtle to the most material, comprised in a separate unity or 'little world'. This idea has been revived in recent years in the Anthropic Principle, which seeks to explain our ability to understand everything in the universe on the grounds that all cosmic realities are present to some degree in each human individual.

The Monads which Leibniz speaks of are beings of this kind. He does not call them embodied souls or microcosms because for him the soul is a special kind of Monad which has the power of reason. Nevertheless, every Monad contains a representation of the universe, with or without rationality, even if it is of a very low order, as with the consciousness of an insect, for example. Anyone who is unfamiliar with the philosophy of Leibniz, and wishes to understand his idea of the Monad, would do well to bear in mind the properties of soul and world-representation. Leibniz also says that the monads have no 'windows' through which they could communicate with one another, as though each were a separate little world or island universe in a way which excluded all the others.

This rather strange-sounding statement highlights an important aspect of the idea of identity which I have just been referring to. Physically-manifest interaction and communication between individuals is something we are constantly aware of, but this is not the thing Leibniz is denying. If body and soul are, so to speak, the 'downstairs' and 'upstairs' components of identity respectively, it will appear that all interaction is by means of the body, or of the physical ego to be more exact, but not by means of the soul as such. This is because our physical self or 'I' is by definition an object *contained* within a larger system of other similar beings, whereas the soul, being the container of our representations of the physical world, cannot stand in anything like the same relation to other beings as the physical ego does. This can be seen from the fact that this ego can never be more than a fraction of any relational activity it enters into (in a one-to-one it is just fifty percent, etc.), whereas the *whole* of this activity is comprised in the soul of each of those who take part in it.

There is thus an essential disproportion between our physical and our psychical ways of relating to the world. The physical is immanent because, along with the body itself, it is in the same category as the things it relates to, while the second is transcendent, because the soul is not in the same category as these objects. The real self consists of both of these realities, the immanent and the transcendent, and it is this transcendent part which Leibniz says has no communication with any other like itself. This may still appear to some people to contradict actual experience, since communication must *originate* in the transcendent part of the person, even though the body or ego is instrumental for it. Nevertheless, the whole process, from mind through sensible signs and back again, is contained by the soul or Monad.

Our thoughts are mostly conditioned by the aspect of communication which strikes both sense and imagination, and that is inevitably the immanent kind. The transcendent position and function of the soul, on the other hand, can only be understood conceptually, since it has nothing that the imagination could depict, which is why it is usually ignored. (Those who ignore this transcendent part of human identity may misunderstand much about human behavior. What is taken for lack of understanding or of good will, for example, might in fact be simply the effect of something which no one has any power over, a part of the self possibly accessible only to God.)

Relations to Platonism and to Mysticism

Plato's philosophy is dualistic in regard to the distinction between the realms of Being and of Becoming, and then between that of body and soul as a consequence of that. For Plato, the soul possesses the real agency of the person, and it is to it that the body is subject, along with its activities. The soul would be in this case the real man or woman, and the body is their means of expression. The negative view of the body which appears here is not only owing to the fact that the body is perceived to be under the soul's control, but also to the fact that the senses are never able to bring us any reality which is stable and uniform enough to constitute truth, rather than opinion or more or less educated guesswork. For Plato, the sense-world of the body is a scene of constant confusion in which knowledge can never be arrived at. But unlike the body, the soul can divert its energies away from the world of sense and communicate with the eternal ideas or Forms. As part of the world of Being, the Forms and their relations are both exact and permanent, unlike sensory objects, whence they can be known truly.

Such is Plato's version of the idea of the soul's transcendence. While it is different, it is still compatible with the view of it which has been discussed already. The idea that the material world is not fully real, because it is in constant change and instability, is complementary to the idea that what we know of it is only by a personal representation, the adequacy of which can vary a great deal from one person to another. From either point of view, therefore, we could employ Plato's answer to the delusions of sense, namely, that the most authentic realities are the Forms, which the mind can grasp without any need for representation, and without any interference from physical change and corruption. The concept of world-representation in the soul corresponds clearly to the realm of imitations which Plato represents as the shadows on the wall of the cave.

One consequence of this conception is that comparisons with physical phenomena will be of little use when explanations of the soul's activities have to be given. For example, there is an Oriental allegory of the soul as a candle-flame which gets passed on from one candle to another. Now if the dualistic conception of the soul is correct, all processes which take place between material things must be equally contained in the soul's own substance, rather as the projected images of a film are contained in the film itself. This implies a very radical difference between the reality proper to the soul itself and the things known to it, and this is why analogies like that of flames or drops of water in the sea must be far less meaningful than is usually thought, when applied to the development of the soul. What relevance they do have is owing to the part played in our identity by the body, and not by the soul as such.

One noteworthy difference between them appears in the fact that, for the physical level of being, the alternatives of staying the same or becoming something else are hard alternatives; it always has to be the one or the other. For soul-life, on the other hand, it is just the opposite, since remaining itself while becoming other things is what it largely consists in; the soul can be said to become whatever it knows. Since real analogies connect only things in similar categories, there can therefore be no reliable analogies between the soul and the things it forms representations of, which are part of its own internal conversation.

Relations to Ethics, Religion, and the Arts

It now remains to add a little about the implications of dualistic thought for ethics, religion, and the arts. The relation of the soul to its world, as just described, affects moral values because it forms an ontological discontinuity between the self or soul and the objects and activities of the world. The transcendent property of the soul could not be confounded with the physical ego and its activities in the outside world without making an impossible combination. Two quite different levels of being would in effect be equated in an illusory manner, and this is what lies at the heart of moral evil; something in the represented world taken to have as much or more importance as the self in which it is represented.

Actions will only be morally right when they respect the difference between the transcendent and the immanent self in those who are involved in them. Conversely, moral evil typically results from a kind of forgetfulness and passional self-identification with something which is not of the same order as the true self.[6] One can see a similar conception of the origin of moral evil in a story in the Hindu scriptures. At the beginning of the world, the gods and demons were being taught about the true self by a discussion. The first possibility considered was that this self was one and the same as the body. Once this was said, the king of the demons would hear no more, and went away telling everyone that this was indeed what the true self was. Thus was born what they called the 'doctrine of the demons', which we know as common-sense materialism.

The illusory sense of self which gives rise to evil can also be said to arise when the will's choices harden into unthinking compulsions. When this condition is dominant, it gives rise to what could deservedly be called the 'cosmic illusion'. The idea of an illusory identification of the self applies to the self in relation to things peripheral to itself or not personal at all, while the self-identifications involved in personal relationships, on the other hand, may or may not fall into this category. The more the relationship is based on shared values, the more free it must be from being a part of the

6. In a standard example of moral wrong like that of stealing, it can be seen that this involves an identification of the self and its wellbeing with an external object, which goes so far as to apparently justify the sacrifice of other peoples' interests. Even where the thing stolen is felt to be a matter of life and death, the identification of the self with it still cannot be justified on a dualistic basis, because what dies could not include the transcendent part of the self which belongs to the soul.

cosmic illusion, because there would then be no question of self-identification with anything of a lower nature than that of the real self. In this connection it is noteworthy that Kant's moral principle that all persons, including oneself, must be treated as ends and never as means, is in line with the moral consequences of soul and world-representation.

The aesthetic realm is as much affected by this conception as the moral realm, as befits the proximity of the beautiful to the good. Dualistic philosophy is relevant to the arts because it relates directly to the claim that great works of art manifest a greater truth and reality than is possible for most people to grasp unaided. If such claims for great art are valid, it will most likely be true that creative artists have a richer and more powerful way of representing reality, and their art will be a means of sharing this greater insight. On the other hand, if the dualist conception of soul and world was mistaken, and we all grasped reality itself all the time, there would presumably be no possibility of anyone having a superior vision or insight. This would certainly be more democratic, and then it would only be possible to say that the artists's vision was different from that of the majority in ways that were more or less interesting. (Exactly how we *could* differ about reality in any case, let alone make mistakes about it, is a problem one must leave to the creative talents of anti-dualists.) Even the greatest works would be only displays of eccentricity, made with some technical skill, but no more than that; they would simply be forms of entertainment.

Finally, it can be seen that the denial of the dualist point of view in today's culture also means in practice an increased pressure on everyone to see their identity only on the physical level. The physical part of identity is necessarily dwarfed and dominated by the physical world it is part of, and as a result, the meaning and value of the individual person has come to appear increasingly dubious. That, too, has negative consequences for religion, because religious beliefs and moral values presuppose that each person is indeed of ultimate importance. We thus grow more depotentiated as persons by this new attitude despite all the new powers that come from technology.

To see oneself simply as one more object in a world of objects is not merely a deluded perception, it is also one which conflicts with our deepest personal reality. Such is the inner conflict which Existentialism has made endless efforts to resolve, and which have failed because it refuses to recognize any personal reality beyond the ego. For such minds, the real meaning of the centrality of man in his universe must be without meaning.

The consequences of the reasoning presented above could hardly be more far-reaching. The conclusion that all perception depends on the intentionality of the perceiver, such that it is inherently a creative act, rules out all systems which deny the reality of the person, because they all depend on the idea that experience is caused by an external reality which is self-subsistent in the identical form in which we perceive it, whether it be material or subtle. In reality, science, culture, religion, the world itself as we know it, depend on the creative intentionality which is sustained by the energies of the soul of the individual. The essential building-blocks of the universe must in this case be not things, but centers of cognition and creative energy. Here is the central issue common to both spirituality and personal identity.

The implication of this, that individual being is one of the eternal verities, may appear at first sight to conflict with the view of it taken by most spiritual doctrines. But this is not so for two reasons: firstly, because the individual and the universal are not alternatives, since each is derived from the other; secondly, because in orthodox teachings, God gives Himself to man as far as that is possible, and it is only possible to the extent that the individual being is a world-containing entity with endless extension as described above, because even omnipotence cannot give itself to nothing. In short, there must be some common measure between the recipient and the received. When the human state is seen in this light, it will not be difficult to proceed to the idea of man as God's mediator in the world.

3

Between God and Nature

The Role of Mediation

The idea that the higher possibilities of the human state can culminate in a state of being which is the third force or mediator between God and nature is one which can readily be explained in terms of the ternary and quaternary relationships between God, man, Providence, and nature. This mediation should not be confused with the theological teaching according to which Christ is the Mediator between God and mankind, because there is a difference of level and of meaning here. The mediation by mankind between God and nature is a special part of the universal hierarchy or Great Chain of Being, whereas the mediation of Christ as Redeemer is both the prototype of man's cosmic mediation, as well as being the revealed basis of salvation. It is part of the spiritual relation between God and man, from which the latter obtains the grace to accede to his position in the universal order and make it effective. Thus the Christian form of this universal doctrine would elaborate it to God-Christ-Man-Nature, but the conclusions about man's cosmic role would remain the same.

When mankind is spoken of as the Mediator, this does not refer primarily to the physical individual, or the physical collectivity. While our embodied state is involved in this role, it is principally the human state as the one in whose soul the whole of creation is represented, because this is what gives mankind the potential for it. What has been said about man as microcosm shows how he holds the point of balance between the worlds of the spirit and of matter.

This union of two natures and of two orders of reality belongs to the essence of what we are created to be, and it is not accidental that the relations this involves can be expressed in numerical and geometrical terms. The mathematical relations between lines and spatial forms is in itself a manifestation of the relations which exist between beings which are far more universal than visible quantities. Consequently, the Ternary and the Quaternary are two fundamental numerically-based relationships which manifest the archetypal relationships between many realities in both the spiritual and the physical realms.

In particular, they apply to and govern the inner constitution of the human state, together with its position in regard to God and the various orders of creation. In order to explain these things, I shall refer to some things said about them by René Guénon in his book *The Great Triad*,[1] and also by Fabre d'Olivet, whose works Guénon makes use of. The Quaternary results from the fact that there are two different kinds of Ternary, as Guénon shows.

The first kind of Ternary is the more metaphysical of the two, as it is one in which the first term has some kind of superiority over the other two, which result from it. It can be represented by an upright triangle (see figure 1) in which the two points on the ends of its base

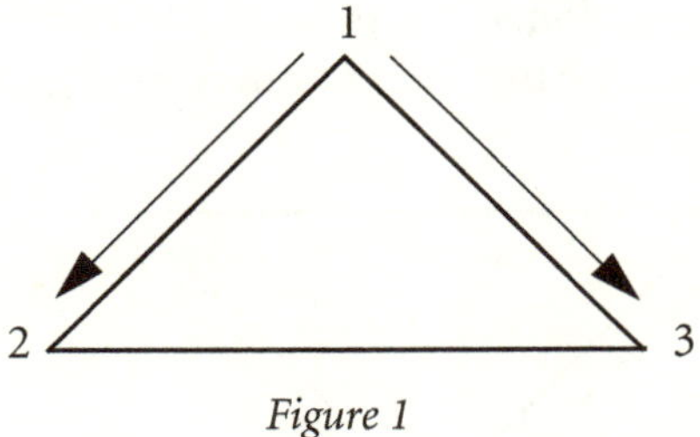

Figure 1

both proceed equally from its apex. A possible example of this would be the Trinity, in which the second and third Persons both proceed from the Father. It also applies to the three Hypostases of Neoplatonism, which are not so much God as the primary realities

1. *The Great Triad* (Hillsdale, NY: Sophia Perennis, 2004).

which proceed from God, although there is a clear inequality between the *Nous* and the World Soul. Nevertheless, these two resultant terms are both implicit in the One, and are distinct realities when manifest.

Other examples of this kind of Ternary abound in nature and religion. It appears that kingship and priesthood are both implicit in prophethood (as appears from the Old Testament), and derive from the latter as two simpler and more specialized realities. In geometry, there are a number of three-dimensional forms which give rise to two others when they are reduced to two dimensions. For example, a cone gives rise to a triangle and a circle by this means; a cylinder gives rise to a circle and a rectangle; a cube to a square and a hexagon; and a spheroid to an ellipse and a circle. More generally still, the laws of quantity give rise to the two realms of arithmetic and geometry. In physics, there are important phenomena which are manifest and treatable both as waves and as particles, as in the case of light, for example. One and the same planet, especially Venus, can give rise to both a morning star and an evening star. In the living world, the archetypal Species usually cannot manifest itself in physical form except as the male and female halves of it.

The second and less metaphysical kind of ternary is more easily seen to be a part of creation. It is represented by an inverted triangle (see figure 2) in which the two upper terms converge downwards to

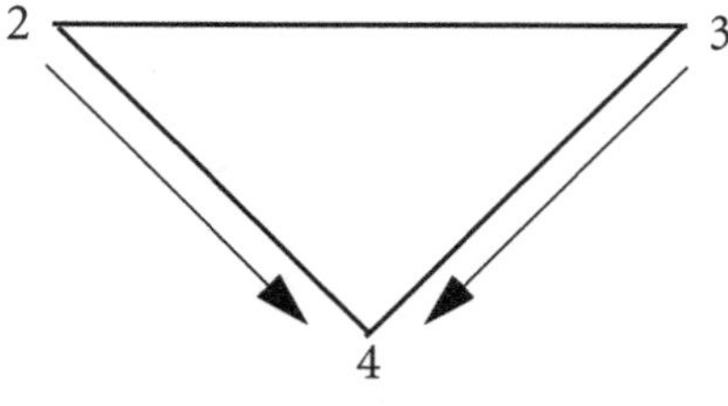

Figure 2

their resultant at the apex. The most obvious example of this is the relation of father, mother, and child. Besides, binary combinations on the chemical level which result in a third compound are only too numerous. One striking natural example of this Ternary is the way the rainbow results from rain and sunlight. On another level, fire and water give rise to steam. Another example is the way the orbital motion of planets and satellites results from linear motion and a force of attraction to a fixed point. A more subtle example in this class is that of knowledge, as every act of knowing results from a relation between the two primaries, the knower and the known.

If the difference between the two kinds of ternary relation is kept in mind, we shall be able to see how the Quaternary results from some among them. It depends on a combination of a ternary as in figure 1, where elements 2 and 3 derive from element 1, and another one as in figure 2, where element 4 derives from elements 2 and 3, the latter being the same in both ternaries. If the upper line of the inverted triangle is joined to the base of the upright one, elements 2 and 3 are common to both, and the result is quadrilateral relating the four elements (see Figure 3) and showing how 4 results directly

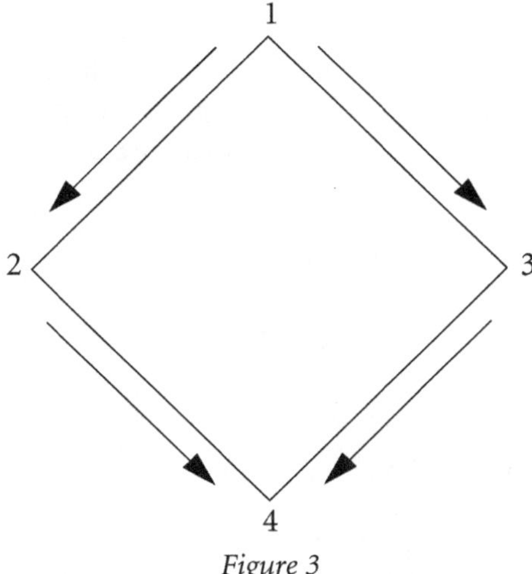

Figure 3

from 2 and 3 and indirectly from 1. If this were applied to living creatures, 1 would be the archetype of the species, 2 and 3 would be the male and female members of the physically instantiated species, while 4 would be their new-born offspring. The fourth element is in a sense a recapitulation of the first on a lower level, which also has some bearing on the meaning of childhood in relation to God.

The Fourfold Being

However, the four most universal realities which are related in this manner are known to both Pythagorean and Far-Eastern teachings under different names, these being God, Providence (or universal spirit), Nature (or fate), and Man (or universal soul). According to this scheme, Providence and Nature both proceed from God, while man is as it were the child of Providence and Nature, though he is no less a creature of God at the same time. This peculiarity of human origin is also indicated by the account in Genesis where Adam and Eve are only created on the sixth day of creation, last of all beings. On this basis, the human being can be taken to be resultant of the divine action and the created natural order as a whole. Because of this relation to creation as a whole, the human state is understood to be an epitome or microcosm of all being, so that each person (the fourth order of being) will be composed of the same things as the 'three worlds,' namely the providential or archetypal world, the psychical or subtle world, and the material world. This is the three-fold inner structure which Fabre d'Olivet represents by the Intellective, Animic, and Instinctive spheres in the structure of the human soul.

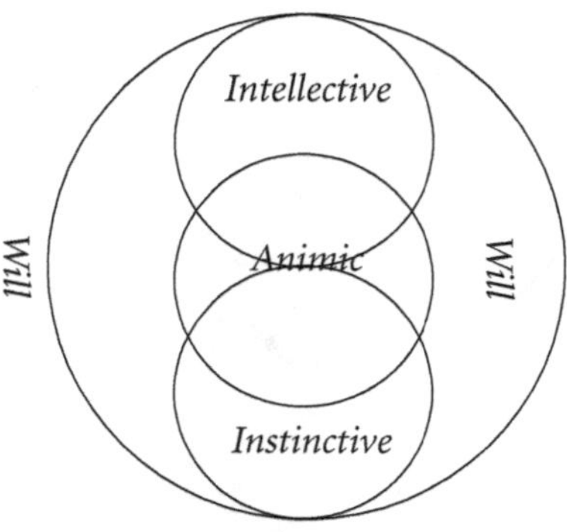

Figure 4

These spheres are represented by four circles (see figure 4), three of which stand on a vertical line, while the fourth surrounds these three. The lowest circle of the three represents the life of instinct which attaches to the body, ruled only by pleasure and pain, because its higher possibilities depend on its participation in those of the soul. The central one represents what is most typically the soul, the realm of the emotions, which are roused by the sense of good and bad. The third circle is that of intellect, which is activated by truth and falsehood.

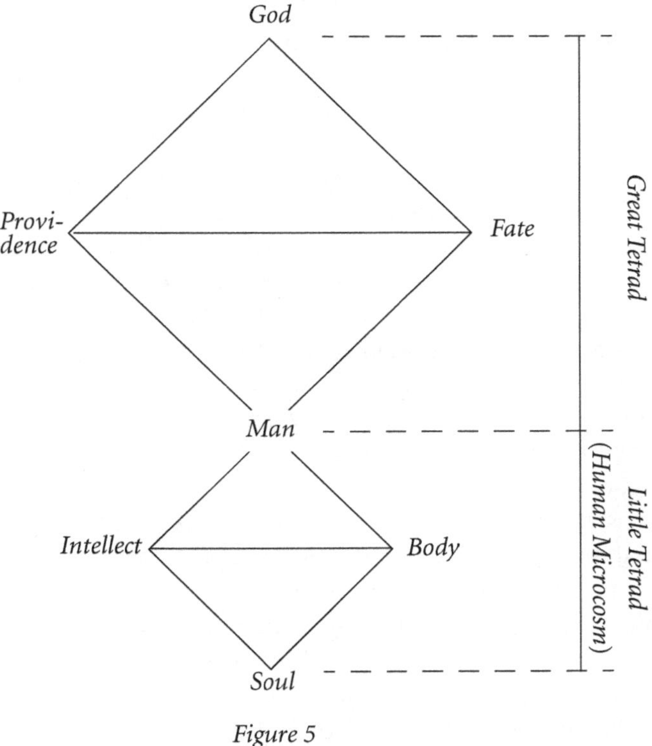

Figure 5

All conscious activity is distributed among these three, in all kinds of combinations and proportions. Their combined effect is what determines the movement of the fourth circle, which represents the will of the whole person. At birth, the soul or self is almost wholly identified with the Instinctive sphere, and it is only through the development of the possibilities of this sphere that it is able finally to trigger the development of the second, or 'Animic' sphere, which is that of soul as such. Similarly, the development of life through the Animic opens up the possibilities of the Intellective sphere. This development can be represented in terms of Figure 4 as an expansion of the Animic sphere to the point where it strikes the center of the Intellective, which then begins its own expansion. Human beings are thus unique in being made up of a union of material, psychical, and noetic principles, reflecting the whole order of creation in miniature. In effect, the soul's activity evolves from a level inferior to the one specific to it, through that of its intrinsic nature, and up to one above its own level, in which it participates in the intellect as the body participates in the soul.

This account of our inner formation is capable of being shown as another quaternary relationship, which reflects the universal one. The fourth circle, representing the will of the person, relates to body, soul, and intellect in ways that reflect the relation of God to Providence, Nature (or Macrocosm), and Man (see figure 5). There are thus two tetrads with Man as the common term: these could be called the Great and the Little Tetrads respectively, and which show the correspondences between Providence and Intellect, between Nature or Fate and the body, and between God and man. One thing this figure does not show is that these relations are dynamic, and in no way static, since the human will is able to strengthen or weaken the relationships it has to each of the three inner spheres, and create different combinations among them.

Unless there was such a being as man, comprising both archetypal and material reality at once, Providence and Fate (or nature) would have no means of relating to one another. It is thus a question of man's being a natural or universal 'pontifex' or bridge-builder, therefore, so long as it is understood that this function is a potentiality in need of realization, which Fabre d'Olivet expresses as follows:

> At the moment when man arrives on earth he belongs to Fate, which leads him captive for a long time in the vortex of fatality. But although he is immersed in this vortex and subject at first to its influence just like all the elementary beings, he bears a divine seed within him which can never be entirely confounded with

> it.... When this seed is fully developed, it constitutes the Will of Universal Man, one of the three great powers of the universe.[2]

Guénon points out that this mediating role of mankind in the cosmos is the macrocosmic equivalent of the mediating role of the soul in each human being, where it relates to and connects the intellect and the body. All this is of fundamental importance for the freedom of the will. If we start from the complex nature of the person, as above, and bear in mind that the Instinctive, Animic, and Intellective 'spheres' are by no means bound to act in concert, but can modify the will by the equivalent of rotation at various speeds, both with and contrary to one another, there will be more than enough to support the idea of free will.

The loss of such ideas from modern philosophy has resulted in a point of view which is too simplified to correspond to reality. Its reasonings about free will are therefore based on the most minimal assumptions about human nature which ignore its internal levels of being. When the person is thus treated as a single subject who knows and wills, moreover, the discussion is biased against free will from the start, because, in nature, the simpler the structure, the less room there is for freedom. Simplistic thought is inherently deterministic; the simplest structure of all, like that of a stone, has no freedom at all.

A Parting of Ways

This interior complexity means that each person has the means to unite himself or herself in an equally natural way to either the Providential or the Fatidic order. However, we do not apply the term 'free will' to both of these options, because what we understand by freedom does not belong to nature, where all is subject to efficient causality, but rather to Providence which comprises the archetypes or formal causes of all that belongs to nature. This is said to be free because it comprises the essential realities of the world as they are

2. See Fabre d'Olivet, 'Histoire du Genre Humain', Introductive, §IV (Paris: Éditions Traditionnelles, 1979), p68 (author's translation).

'before' being instanced in material form and so subjected to all kinds of constraint.

The soul which aligns itself with Providence, and therefore with freedom, will thus be the one which realizes the possibilities of the spiritual nature to the fullest extent possible for the individual concerned. This involves an orientation of the whole person which is not to be confused with the divisive effects of an unintegrated intellectuality which is made an end in itself, and so denies its spiritual and sacramental role. On the contrary, it applies to the body as well, by its participation in the soul, which in turn participates in intellect; it too is spiritualized in its own way, therefore. Concerning the effects of this union, Guénon says: 'In uniting itself to Providence and consciously collaborating with it, the human will can become a counter-balance to destiny and finally neutralize it.' In the words of Fabre d'Olivet,

> The harmony of the Will and Providence constitutes Good; Evil is born of their opposition. Man has received three forces adapted to each of the three modifications of his being... and the unity which binds them [these forces], that is to say Man, is perfected or depraved, according as it tends to become blended with the Universal Unity or to become distinguished from it.[3]

In other words man approaches either perfection or depravity depending on which of the two poles of manifestation he gravitates towards: the pole of unity or the pole of multiplicity.

This also makes it easier to see how each soul can choose its own destiny, since the inward relations it makes with its material, psychical, and spiritual possibilities are in effect the formal causes of its relations to the external conditions under which it lives and develops. In other words, it is not so much a matter of the person being modified by a set of conditions as of a soul gravitating to a set of conditions which correspond to its interior relations, and under which the latter will be best able to realize their potential. This leads

3. 'Examinations of the Golden Verses', §12 (New York: Thorsons, 1975), pp54–55, and *The Great Triad* (Hillsdale, NY: Sophia Perennis, 2004), chap. 21, 'Providence, Will, and Destiny'.

to certain questions about the will which are hardly ever treated theoretically, particularly concerning the distinction between the things we do and the things we suffer. If the movement of the will is based on the component wills of the Instinctive, Animic, and Intellectual principles, it can be seen that the adverse wills which confront us need only be the counterparts of unintegrated acts of volition within us.

Like wills can only connect with like, but if the whole person is harmonized in relation to the intellective principle, the will must be free, and so not liable to attract adverse volition to itself, having none within. The choice of freedom and free will outlined above is implicitly obedience to the will of God, where the universal Divine will can be discerned by means of the threefold constitution of the being. Its implication is that each person is born with a destiny to develop as much as possible through the Instinctive, Animic, and Intellective levels, with the grace of sacred tradition.

This is not merely in the interests of the individuals concerned, and their personal freedom, but it is also for the greater good of the world, since it is only through such persons that nature as a whole can connect with its archetypal causes, and thereby with God. This union between God and nature ensures that the natural order functions in a regular and benign manner. Conversely, as mankind fails to realize the role as Mediator, natural forces grow increasingly violent and chaotic, and disasters become frequent. The Apocalypse is the final extreme of this disorder.

Such is the relation upon which natural harmony and order among the elements depends. This universal destiny is necessarily adversely affected by the Fall. For 'unfallen' humanity, it would have been spontaneous and would have been wholly self-motivating. In the fallen state, however, there is much less, or even none, of the will to fulfil this destiny, so that individuals may often be content to remain even at the instinctive level if conditions allow. This is why in the actual world this higher evolution usually does not take place, except where individuals are subject to relentless external pressures which force them onto the battlefield, so to speak. As time passes, this kind of growth becomes slower on average, until it is still deficient even in later life.

The deepening identification between the soul and the intellective principle, which mediates between the human and the Divine, is of course a union with an eternal reality. As such, it should obviously amount to what is meant by the immortality of the soul, especially as union with Providence must mean a deliverance from Fate. Mortality belongs explicitly to Fate, since alternate aggregation and decay are its typical operations.

For Guénon, however, personal immortality seems to be no more possible for those who unite with Providence than for those who unite with Fate. There are two reasons for this: firstly it is because his idea of the soul is conditioned by its role in occultism, where one is concerned with the 'subtle body,' which is defined as a quasi-material intermediary between the personal soul and the body. Following this materialized view of 'soul', Guénon expresses the view that the soul, just like the body, is an aggregate of elements drawn from its surrounding world, as in fact is the case with the 'subtle body'.

Secondly, Guénon's position is determined by his belief that there could be only one real being, which he refers to as the 'Principle'. But the idea implicit in this, that a totally exclusive reality must enhance that of the Principle is in any case logically groundless. To think in this way is to betray a suspicion that the higher reality must be exclusively real because it may have no power to generate any other kind of reality. At the same time, he maintains that the individual person is what results when the Principle intersects a certain plane of existence, although this interaction would inconsistently imply that the Principle and the plane are both phenomena which have enough in common to be able to interact. He also speaks of a 'passage' from one plane of existence to another without explaining what it is that thus passes. One is left with a supposed interaction of a reality which is beyond the need for salvation with a relative being which is incapable of it. It would, however, be foolish to ignore what is profitable for the soul in these truths about its universal status, when the alternative is merely an equation of Truth with itself.

Further Numerical Symbolism

Finally, there is another aspect of this subject which reveals a close parallelism between Pythagoreanism and Far-Eastern tradition which is referred to in *The Great Triad*,[4] though the explanation offered for the squaring of the numbers is very cryptic. This appears in the way that the 3-4-5 right-angled triangle is used by both traditions to symbolize the way in which the human Will in union with Providence can prove equal to Fate. Providence is represented by 3, because 3 is the first symbolic numerical unity after Unity itself, as befits the first reality in order after God. Man, or the human Will, is represented by 4, because this will is the fourth principle in which the Instinctive, Animic, and Intellective are integrated. Fate is represented by 5, because 5 is the 'first multitude' and so symbolically the origin of multiplicity. In Far-Eastern symbolism it represents Earth, while 6 represents Heaven.

In the 3–4–5 triangle, however, the sides corresponding to 3 and 4 total 7, and so obviously exceed 5 between them, so that they only equal 5 when all the sides are squared, as in $9 + 16 = 25$. This raises the question of the symbolic aspect of the power to which the numbers are raised. The raising of a series of numbers to different powers appears in the Platonic Lamda, with its series 1, 2, 4, 8 and 1, 3, 9, 27, that is to say, 1, 2^1, 2^2, 2^3, and 1, 3^1, 3^2, 3^3. In either group, 1 would result from a zero index, e.g., $2^0 = 3^0 = 1$ The unit is common to both and is any number to the power of zero. The indices are therefore 0, 1, 2, and 3. The zero power represents all realities as they are in God 'before' any kind of creation. Where it is 1, the realities represented by 3, 4, and 5 are at the level of archetypal reality. Here, Providence and Man clearly outweigh Fate, as is shown by the way the sum of 3 and 4 exceeds 5. In the human microcosm, this 3 corresponds to the Intellective sphere.

Conversely, at the lowest extreme of instantiation in matter, the relation between these three appears as $3^3 + 4^3$ or 27 and 64, making 91, while 5^3 makes 125, so that at this level Nature or Fate must dominate the other two. In man, this corresponds to the Instinctive

4. Chap. 21.

sphere. Intermediate between these two levels is the realm of subtle or psychic reality, to which the Animic sphere corresponds, and here the index applied must be 2. It is also here that Providence and the Will together can balance Fate, as represented by $3^2 + 4^2 = 5^2$ or $9 + 16 = 25$. This applies to the highest level of creation as *natura naturata*, where it is joined to its Divine origin by man's Will united to Providence.

At this level, then, it is not a question of absolute superiority over Nature or Fate, but of an equality which can imply a richer and more prolific possibility than superiority alone could imply, because it must include a mutuality enriching both sides of the relation; nature is spiritualized as its possibilities are able to reach their highest perfection, and the soul shares in another range of realities while remaining true to its own.

4

The Role of Ideas in Free Will

A Property of Human Consciousness

Since those who acknowledge the existence of ideas outnumber those who believe in free will, it would be fortunate if the freedom of the will could be shown to be connected with the presence of ideas in us. It would be even better if the very source of free will lay, arguably, in ideas, the consciousness of *natura naturans*, or the formative principles of sensory objects. The existence of ideas means that man knows not only things, but also the ideas of them, such that for him all reality is doubled. Animal consciousness relates only to sense-objects, and derives its characteristics from that. Only by means of ideas can we both engage with things *and* stand back from them at the same time.

Having ideas of things, we can form innumerable new combinations of the things we know by their ideas, and from among these combinations we can choose the ones which make for the best use of their objects from our own point of view. This stage of the argument applies whether the ideas are subsistent Forms, as they are according to Plato, or whether they are just images which are less real than their material objects, as they are for empiricists.

By means of ideas, which duplicate all objects, we can in effect go behind the screen of natural appearances, so as to re-order them. The vision of new possibilities which ideas make possible is the reason why human beings can make innovative changes, while animals cannot. The last animal of a species spends its life doing exactly the same things as were done by the first one. Only man does not have to keep on doing the same things *ad infinitum*, regardless of their value. Having rearranged our ideas of persons, things, and activities as much as we can, it may still result that the best we can do is to act in the same way as before, but now our outwardly inflexible activity is inwardly free. Conversely, a bad use of ideas will result in changes which would be for the worse. In this case, there is an outward freedom, expressed in creative change, but inwardly it is unfree, because it is worse than no change at all.

This points to the other main basis of freedom. The re-combinations that are made by means of ideas must be intelligent if they are to realize freedom. Intelligence involves insight into the essential natures of the ideas which the will is manipulating. The practical success this leads to shows that ideas are far from fabrications of the mind to enable us to label and classify things. Things and their ideas have inflexible natures, which means that some combinations the will makes of them harmonize with the essential natures of the things in question, while most others do not. The possibility of unrealistic combinations of ideas illustrates the point that ideas as mental images are not subject to the natural laws that govern their objects, whence their profusion of possibilities.

Where reality is resistant to attempted recombinations, it is always owing to a failure to understand what kinds of relations things can have, no matter whether they be physical or whether as ideas. Thus, while ideas are a necessary condition for free will, they are not a sufficient one, since their intrinsic natures have to be understood. Freedom therefore depends on both ideas and intelligence, and intelligence must work on two levels, those of insight into essential natures, and of devising the different systems of relationships that can be formed among them. The latter function without the former is a guarantee of disaster.

The fact that human reality is divided between things and ideas-of-things means that there are two fundamentally different, but closely related, realms in which the will can operate. The interval between them is in effect the opening through which all possibilities of physical determination of human wills escape irrecoverably. The lack of free will which can be seen in animals results from the fact that their wills relate only to objects in the outside world. Thus they can only engage with the things they experience by merging themselves with their functions and mode of being, so sharing in the same unfreedom. If they could be said to travel along a single track, man could be said to travel along two tracks as well as across the region between them. This is the equivalent of an extra dimension.

This means that rational action is always preceded by a symbolic overview of it, which is relevant where moral responsibility is concerned. In such cases, the will is moved by mental images which represent the object in question. Since the will as such can only be moved by the ideas of objects and not by the objects themselves, it must needs be exempt from the physical causality which applies to things in the external world. Moral responsibility results from this lack of physical necessity.

This consideration of responsibility is made only in respect of ideas, and not of the other condition, that of intelligence, however. While moral responsibility on a basis of ideas alone is perfectly evident, it can be modified by the role of the intelligence, depending on its adequacy. The better the potential action is understood, the greater the responsibility, as intelligence necessarily enhances freedom. A greater intelligence allows a greater insight into alternative and more constructive possibilities, so that its choice of harmful ones will be the more culpable. This could easily lead to the classic paradox that actions which do not contain the full conditions for free will cannot be culpable, however much harm they may bring about. However, bad actions which lack intelligence normally result from a failure to use an intelligence which one really has. Such negligence proves an absence of good will. This gives such cases a parity of culpability with that of cases where intelligence is used, but in a perverse manner.

The images formed on computer screens are a class of external objects which function in very much the same way as our mental images of things, and for this reason the use of them is experienced as an enhancement of freedom. Here again the application of intelligence is an essential factor. One can perform on the screen a juggling with different possibilities which is very much like what we do with our ideas. This example underlines the point that freedom largely depends on the ability to symbolize possibilities and rearrange them in a form which is easy to handle. Whether in the mind or in the computer, we prescind from concrete reality so as to be able to re-enter it on more favorable terms, and our moral responsibility is implicit in this power of control.

The Will and Physical Causes

Supposing there was a proof that our actions really were caused directly by natural forces, just as heat causes the boiling of water: in this case we should still be able to have an idea or mental image of ourselves and the agencies controlling us. This would mean that the relationship between ourselves and the external cause would be known to us according to a mode of being fundamentally different from that of the cause or agency itself; a single-nature entity without self-reflection would be acting on one with a dual nature. In reality, external control is only effective where the controlling agent and the controlled are of the same nature, but persons may approximate to this if their awareness is sufficiently defective.

Those who believe in determinism, and do their best to convince others of it, do not see that they are absurdly lending their help to a controlling power which by definition leaves no power outside itself. The mere fact that we continue to have an independent point of view means that we can judge whether the things we are doing are according to our will or not. If they are, the hidden controller would only be making us do what we want to do anyway, and control is not needed. (If our likes and dislikes were similarly created from outside, there would be no self to be controlled.) When our activities and state of being are not according to our will, however, it is just as possible to show how they result from previous applications of our wills as when our condition is according to our will.

Returning to the role of ideas in free will, and the fact that the will is moved by ideas of things, it is clear that part of the function of ideas is to break the continuity of physical causality where it affects the will. This can be summed up by the principle that *every causal chain with which the will is involved can only act on with the will outside its own sequence*, that is, in the mental sequence which represents it.

This intervention by ideas between stimulus and response means that all, or nearly all, human actions are causeless, at least as science understands causes. There is no end of examples to show that ideas or mental images are not subject to physical laws. A mental drink of water does not quench thirst, while a mental thirst can cease without a mental drink. Mental tortoises can run faster than mental hares, if they wish. Since these mental phenomena are the occasional causes of willed actions, such actions cannot be compelled by natural forces. Physical causes obviously do have an effect on the will, but only in a way which 'inclines without necessitating,' an expression of the Scholastics in regard to the influence of planetary aspects on the will, which does in reality extend to all natural agencies whatever.

For every mental representation or idea there is also the mental negative of it, as where the ideas of working and sleeping, for example, are matched with those of not-working and not-sleeping. These pairings of positives and negatives allow us to judge whether the thing in question is better (under the circumstances) than the absence of it. Physical reality has no equivalent for this property of ideas. On the physical level, working may also be an option, but not-working is simply an unspecific nothing which is the same as any other nothing. This is another property of ideas which distinguishes them from the things they are ideas of.

The fact that all physical causes must pass through the non-physical realm of ideas also means that the ideas one has of them can be ordered in ways which are not tied to their powers as physical causes. In this non-physical realm, the nearest thing to physical causality which they can exert is the power of sympathy or attraction which they can arouse in the mind and will. But in all such cases, the power they have over the will is always 'voluntary' inasmuch as it acts by the mental consent of the will to its mental representations. Only if the will complies with a causal input until this response becomes automatic, will the result be something like physical necessity, at least in appearance. This could be called 'voluntary compulsion'.

In such cases, there may be no awareness that the will is allowing itself to be operated on as though it were a physical entity, at least not until some problem results. This condition is one which Gurdjieff calls 'mechanicalness', a condition close to the inflexible unfreedom of natural causes. To become aware of the ways in which one's will is allowing itself to work, or rather, be worked, is one of the hardest spiritual problems. Wills may be free, but in practice they are a lot less free than they should be. The endless possibilities contained in the freedom of the will include the paradoxical one that the will can habitually act as though it were not free. If, as Fabre D'Olivet says, the strength of free will increases in proportion as we exercise it,[1] it must equally decrease with lack of use.

Such is the general principle involved and, if true, need not be any more surprising than that the mind should improve with appropriate use. But what this means in practice for the will is not so clear. Every use of the will involves some degree of freedom by definition, so this exercise of free will must mean the exercise of a higher than normal form of it. The difference between high and low levels of free will can be understood in the light of what was said in Chapter 3, about the Intellective, Animic, and Instinctive levels of the soul's activity. A high level of free will must employ a combination of these three levels thus: an idea or value or ideal in the intellective sphere must arouse an appropriate emotional response in the animic sphere, and that in turn must trigger a corresponding outward action. Where activity is consistently directed on this basis, the person in question is said to be an authentic being. (This is also a major example of the universal action of 'vertical causality', as opposed to the physical kind, acting here in the individual person, and so is under his or her direction.)[2]

The converse of this is the case where the contents of the intellective sphere have little impact on the animic, whose emotional responses are nearly always triggered instead by whatever stimuli happen to be present. In this case, the contents of sense-perception, including the inclinations of other persons, are the causes of one's actions because of their unopposed access to the animic sphere

1. Fabre d'Olivet, 'Histoire Philosophique du Genre Humain', Intro., §IV, p68.

2. See Wolfgang Smith, *The Quantum Enigma*, third edition (Hillsdale, NY: Sophia Perennis, 2005), chap. 6.

which prompts action. Where this condition is dominant, it is that of the inauthentic being, who is failing to exercise free will in any significant manner.

But authenticity by itself is not enough to guarantee that one will be in the truth, however, because the authentic integration of the three 'spheres' of soul-life can still be pathological, varying from the mildly insane to the positively evil. Adolf Hitler is a modern prototype of the evil authentic man: his integration of idea-emotion-action was as sound as it could be in any saint.

A spiritually valid authenticity on the other hand will be relative to the universal values, such as charity, humility, and moral integrity. Values of this kind must be included among whatever other values in the intellective sphere should motivate the authentic person. Because this condition is increasingly ignored, the modern world is afflicted by innumerable authentic beings who are either evil or deranged, or both, but who have all the self-assurance of those who know themselves to be authentic. Such persons account for most of those who are known as 'saints of Satan' in Islamic terminology.

This points to the conclusion that the exercise of the higher free will, which causes it to grow stronger, will involve activities which increase one's authenticity, subject to the moral norms which apply to everyone. To be mediocre is to be a mixture of the authentic and the inauthentic, but the better this is understood, the easier it will be to increase the extent of one's authenticity.

The Self Transcends its World

The difference between the authentic and the inauthentic person can also be understood in terms of the soul's representation of its world. In the former case, the soul has full awareness owing to the conscious relations it has both to the intellect and to the senses, whereas in the latter, self-awareness is stifled by the soul's habitual confusion of itself with the sense-content of its world. Such failures to realize the difference in degree of being between the self and its world reduce the power of free will. When the self puts itself on the same level as that of its own mental contents, or even lower, it is committing the fundamental confusion which I have already called the 'cosmic illusion', because in this case the individual cannot distinguish himself from his 'cosmos', or see himself as anything other than an item in the system which depends on his conception of it. All things under the headings of sins and crimes and vices result inevitably from this confusion. Such things are obviously failures to realize values in practice, because the nodal point or fulcrum of value, the difference in degree between the person and his perceptions, has been lost from his awareness.

Some modern thinkers deny the existence of non-material ideas or mental representations, because they fail to see that we could just as easily (and as absurdly) deny sense-perception as well. Perceptions and ideas are separable for thought, but not in practice, because sensations do not become perceptions until the power of attention develops them into mental images, whether these are understood as consciousness of their Forms, or simply as images. Once our relation to the idea is activated by the sensation, it can be both retained in the memory and re-used in different forms by the imagination. In sense-perception, physical realities trigger the ideas or universals at specific times and places, as there is nothing else by which individual things can be known, and this is why we must deny sense-perception if we deny mental representation.

This does not mean that I am claiming, like Locke, that our knowledge consists wholly of ideas which correspond to the contents of the sense world. In reality the range of ideas in the mind extends far beyond those which correspond to sense-objects. Firstly, there are all those ideas which govern relationships among both concrete and abstract realities. Then there are the higher-order universals, such as Being, Unity, Identity, Proportion. The questions as to whether all ideas are or are not ideas of sense objects, and whether there is any truth in the claim that all knowledge comes through the senses, are thus the very ones which make us aware of the true range of the ideas. There is no necessity for an idea to comprise a sensuous image order to be an idea.

Mental images are subtle intermediaries between sense objects and ideas proper, which are not the same thing as images. If a carpenter has the idea of a chair, his mind derives from it the mental images of particular chairs. The material chair may then be the cause of mental images of itself which we may or may not consciously relate to the chair-idea. The chair-idea, however, far from being an abstraction, has so full a reality that it cannot be manifest in one sensory form or image, but rather needs innumerable such images and their material counterparts to reveal its content. Although the chair-idea relates to a class of sensory objects, therefore, it contains something which goes beyond what is possible for any one material chair. The same applies to the idea which the individual has of himself. While the body and the ego can be represented by mental images, there is much else about the self which cannot be known in this way. The self's idea of itself transcends sensuous content, even though it includes it.

According to the traditional idea of the soul employed by Leibniz, the soul is a simple substance, and therefore not subject to natural causes external to itself. All its actions and modifications are thus self-generated or spontaneous. As the soul or monad contains a representation of the universe, it thereby contains its own form of all the causal agents that could act upon its ego. What connects this with the present argument is the fact that physical forces cannot in any case be 'external' to the ideas of them, because this kind of relation can apply only to things of the same order. Where the person is equated with his ego, rather than with the soul, he would of course be on the same level as external causes, so that we need not expect there to be a free will for the ego when it is separated from self-awareness.

The freedom or spontaneity of the will has already been argued for on the grounds that only it can cause the decisive act, no matter how many other agencies may be pressing on the ego at the same time. In man' s being as a whole, these agencies can only make their presence felt in the form of ideas or representations, so that they are the *occasional causes* of our actions, even though their operation is not physical in itself. They are thus 'causes' of our choices in a weaker and looser sense than that understood by science in relation to the natural order.

In the same text of Leibniz,[3] the soul is said to be characterized by

3. *Leibniz: Philosophical Writings*: 'Metaphysical Consequences of the Principle of Reason,' 8, G.H.R. Parkinson, ed., p175.

the two functions of 'perception' and 'appetition'. The first of these terms applies to ideas, and the second to one's voluntary relations to them. The creative function of the soul lies in the selections it makes among the ideas and the relations it makes or discovers between them, and between them and itself. Thus the will exercises a causality of its own within the monad, as it is the cause of its successive modifications. Similarly, it is the cause of the relations it has to its world and to other souls or monads, since these result from its internal relations. The causality of God on all beings appears in their being brought into existence, and in the manner in which all their activities are coordinated with each other. But God's action is of an internal kind, and no doubt its influence on the individual comes through the 'divine spark' or 'eye of the soul', working by an inward power of attraction.

Two Levels of Freedom

This next part of the subject is based on the role of ideas as subsistent, objective universals, and not as mere images and conventional signs. On the common sense level, free will is a power to choose independently of physical causes among innumerable different objects whose origin, presence and properties our wills may have little power over. This is the level where the operative factor is ideas supported by reason, but without any direct interaction with the supra-individual level. Such free elective decision-making among the contents of experience is traditionally termed *libertas minor*, surprising as this may be to those who never think of free will in any other form.

The reason for this is that the function of the intellect is to judge between created reality or *natura naturata*, and the Forms or *natura naturans*, which are the archetypes of the former. This is where we must depart from the form of argument which treats ideas as just mental images, which suffices for *libertas minor*, remaining, as it does, on the level of phenomena. The Forms are the content of Providence, the divine activity of designing, preserving, and leading all beings to the ends for which they were created. St.Augustine identifies the Forms with Providence where he observes that everything we know by the senses is held together by some numerical determinant, 'without which it will fall back into nothing.' Only through eternal and changeless Forms can changeable things retain their identity through the 'phases of their temporal duration':

> If everything in existence would become nothing, once form was entirely taken away, then this unchangeable form is itself their providence. Through it (Providence) all changing realities subsist so as to achieve their perfection and movements by the numerical principles belonging to their forms.[4]

The sequences of physical causes and effects in the natural world by no means do such positive things. Rather, they bring things into existence and later dissolve them in an automatic manner, subject to the operation of laws which cannot take account of individuals. Such is the realm science is concerned with, and which is traditionally called Fate. Fate is the typical operation of *natura naturata*, and the distinction between it and Providence, to which Fate as a whole is subject, is an essential issue for human beings, who have a place in both, since they are uniquely composed from all realities from the highest of the Forms down to matter. Augustine expresses this microcosmic idea by dividing all beings into three classes: those which simply exist; those which exist and live; and man, who exists, lives, and has knowledge.

Consequently, man has many levels of being in himself, with which he can identify, and he is under no physical necessity to give preeminence to any one in particular. The Forms are in human consciousness what Providence is in the universe, from whence the intellect has an intrinsic relation to Providence, and secondarily, to God. Involvement in the material basis of life is natural and necessary to some degree for everyone, but the fatal aspect of this involvement is counteracted when the will has an additional determination toward God. This kind of preference, when it predominates, realizes a personal relation to Providence, and therefore to the formal causes of the physical processes of the world. The free relation this creates between the individual and the material world

4. *The Free Choice of the Will*, p155, bk. 2, chap. 17, [45] (Washington, DC: Catholic University of American Press, 1968).

is called *libertas major.* This full development of free will has been referred to in Chapter 3 as being the will of Universal Man, which is one of the three universal powers: the 'Great Triad' of Heaven, Earth, and Man. In conjunction with Providence, Man is equal in power to Fate, besides which this state is the common factor in sanctity according to the different traditions.

Here, the orientation of the free will is not toward choices among objects or actions, but toward a condition for which such choices are beyond the pressure of necessity. The will is thus free in a deeper and fuller sense, in a continuous elective act, unlike that of *libertas minor,* which is always short-term, multifarious, and without any intrinsic connection with truth, or with the higher values in general.

Proclus, Plotinus, and Augustine speak in very similar ways about this higher free will under Providence. Proclus distinguishes Providence and Fate on the basis that everything produced by Fate is by a greater priority produced by Providence, but not vice-versa. The consequence is that 'many things escape Fate, but nothing escapes Providence.'[5] The intellect, he says, exists under Providence alone, such that it 'rules over [physical] necessity,' or Fate, while Providence rules even over intellect (ibid., 8). Although man (it is said) is by essence above Fate, he can by 'habitude' become subject to it. Accordingly, man can be ruled by both Providence and Fate, or he can transcend Fate and 'follow Providence alone'.

Plotinus expresses these ideas where he points out that the exercise of the will in the outside world depends on events over which it has no control.[6] On this level, goodness needs bad things to counteract. If virtue itself could choose, it would prefer that occasions did not arise for it to be put into action. The brave would prefer that there were no wars; doctors, that there were no illnesses to be treated; the generous, that there were no one in need, and so on. Given these contingencies, virtue 'becomes a collaborator under compulsion,' and so does not have the 'self-disposal' which is the mark of full free will. By this standard, *libertas minor* is always a freedom diluted with physical necessity, by virtue of the things it relates to.

5. Proclus, *Providence and Fate*, §3, Thomas Taylor tr.
6. Plotinus, *Ennead* VI, 8, 5, MacKenna translation.

Similarly, Augustine says that free will results from adherence to the 'changeless good, which is common to all,' where this common good is said to be that of 'truth and wisdom'. All sin, he says, comes from a turning away from the unchangeable to a changeable good, without necessity,[7] just as Proclus says that the soul can make itself subject to the forces of Fate, to which it is intrinsically superior. This is not to be taken to mean that we are being told to will the spiritual good to the exclusion of everything else, but rather that it should be the principal object of the will, having the highest priority. The willing of the highest good confers new meaning and value on every other kind of good which is also willed.

The predominant direction of the will to truth and wisdom in the whole person has the effect of relating all the different parts of the personality to their ruling principle. Insofar as this kind of personal wholeness is lacking, the spiritual direction of the will loses its cosmic role, which is to raise nature up to God. Just as man cannot realize his most essential possibilities except under the rule of Providence, no more can nature realize its own except in subjection to Providence mediated by humanity.

Free Will in Relation to God

According to theological principles, God is able to act on human wills directly, despite the apparent contradiction from the fact that the will is by definition a cause which is not itself externally caused. This does not mean that it is not caused in its existence, of course, only in its operation. But this can give rise to many absurd misunderstandings as long as God's action on the will is thought of in terms of natural causality, or as the work of another individual agent like oneself. In reality, the Divine action results from the effects of God's simply being known as such. As the highest good, God thus moves the soul by means of its self-motive nature, which responds to all kinds of good. Such is the role of the Unmoved Mover, which does not exclude particular interventions in history,

7. *The Free Choice of the Will*, bk. 2 [53], chap. 19.

where the action is not possible for subordinate agents, and the most important among these are the revealed religions.

This means that the will does not have to be independent of all forms of outside causality in order to be free, but only that it be free from the action of natural causes and of other psychic agents like itself. Its freedom as an uncaused cause could be described as 'relatively absolute' on its own level, therefore. It is in no way reduced by determination by a higher order of causality than its own, any more than where the higher causality determines it to exist.

There is an obvious sense in which man's will is caused, inasmuch as it is created; its essence is clearly not one and the same with its existence. On this basis, it would be true to say that God causes all the acts of human wills *en bloc*, as their Creator, rather as the manufacturers of a car are the cause of all the things that its owner does with it, also *en bloc*. This distinction is important, because this causality does not imply that the manufacturers are causing the owner to drive to any given destination at any given time, even though this event is incorporated in the whole mode of activity which they have produced.

Another conception of causal action on the will is based on an analogy with the function of food in the body or fuel in an engine. In the case of food, its causality gives us the energy to make each of our actions possible, not in their individual natures, but simply *qua* actions. On this level, the power of the will is sustained by natural, not Divine, causes, but its freedom is no more affected by that than in the previous case. In short, man's free will results from his existing at all, because nothing can have being without some causal power as well, and that is the basis of freedom.

However, if God were also the cause of the particular acts of our free will, as is said by those who teach predestination, this would mean that God did not delegate any causal power to created beings. In this case, God would be the only real agent in existence, such that when wood, for instance, appeared to be burned by fire, it would really be burned by God, under the guise or veil of visible fire. But if created beings had no causal power of their own, they could not even be substances, if in fact a measure of independent causal power is a defining characteristic of substance. In the absence of such a power in individual substances, there would be no possibility of interaction between them and God or any other being, as they would be incapable of either receptivity, resistance or response.

In this case, there would be only one real substance, that of God, and the resulting reality would be conceptually that of Non-Dualism or 'substantial monism' as it is called by academic philosophy. In practice, if not in principle, Christian thought veers pragmatically to and fro between precisely this monist position, and a physical dualism, within which man and God confront one another as though they were both creatures. These two extremes create balance in a pragmatic way, as two opposite errors can cancel out, but they both fall short of the metaphysical conception of substance. Neither of these conceptions compels anyone to think beyond the level of concretes. Thus they both treat God simply as an individual agent, and not as the cause of agency itself.

Such inadequate alternatives are transcended in the concept of the 'naturally supernatural', the great chain of being, which allows an answer outside the false dilemmas of thought which is tied to concretes. The question of a causality delegated from God to man is understandable from there being innumerable degrees of being from God down to the detritus of creation. This applies independently of man's being made in the image of God and being susceptible of a full realization of that image. If this state of being is to be effectual, it must involve some sharing in the divine attributes, these including causality.

To maintain the opposite of this, namely, that God is exclusively agent and that man is exclusively patient, is to maintain an absolute and final barrier between God and man, which would subvert orthodox teachings about participation in the divine nature through the Sacraments, denying the implications of man's being made in the divine image. In reality, the closer by nature man is to God, the greater must be his degree of being or substance. This point is made clearly by Aquinas:

> Therefore, that the order of things be complete, those nearest to God, and hence most remote from non-being, must be totally devoid of the potentiality to non-being; and such things are

necessary absolutely. Thus, some created things have being necessarily.[8]

As being and causal power are inseparable for the reason given already, man participates in the attribute of self-subsistence, in his soul if not in his body, in this life. Leibniz expresses this idea by making substance to be a fount of volitional energy. So essential is this to its nature that it could not be otherwise without ceasing to exist. This is what lies behind the statement that 'Substance is a being capable of action.'[9]

This identification between substance and capacity for action is implicit in the way in which Plato argues for the immortality of the soul in the *Phaedrus*, 245C–E. Self-motion is said to be essential to the soul, and for this reason it is the first principle of motion to bodies and to all things that are moved from without. Thus the soul must withdraw from the body when its self-motive nature has no longer any outlet. Without this principle of self-motion, all other forms of motion would soon run down to nothing, and the universe would cease to be.

The self-moved nature is in a higher order than that which is moved only from without, and lower than that which moves everything without being moved either by itself or any other. Thus the self-motive power does not mean that man can transcend creaturehood as such, since what was once created must forever be so, but it does mean that once he has his created being, he could not lose it except by an act of annihilation, as Leibniz expresses it. Such an act is only a theoretical possibility, because God could only uncreate what He has created in response to a change of circumstances which God must by definition be able to foresee.

To draw a firm distinction between the two ideas, that man has a causal power of his own, and that he has not, is at least as reasonable as to distinguish in regard to whether individuals are sinful or not. Conversely, if it were possible to argue that human causal power exists

8. Aquinas, *SCG*, bk. 2, chap. 30, [6].

9. Leibniz, *The Monadology*, 'Principles of Nature and Grace', p406 (Robert Latta edition).

only in appearance, while being really moved by cosmic or divine causality, it would equally be possible to argue that man's sinful behavior was not really his own, but was imposed on him by hidden forces. Besides, any such idea that apparent free will must really be unfree because of unknown forces can be answered on the same basis, to the effect that clear cases of unfree action could just as well be free in reality, because of yet other factors of which we are ignorant.

When ideas of human free will are taken in relation to God, they are always liable to evoke the ancient pseudo-problem that if God has foreknowledge of our actions, we cannot have free will. If our actions really were predetermined, they would of course be foreknowable, but the question is whether the converse is also true.

Augustine answered this by saying that if God can foresee the movements of our will, He must also foresee our having power of it:

> this power will be mine all the more certainly because of the infallible foreknowledge of Him who foreknew that I would have it.[10]

However, there is also a psychological problem here, simply owing to the fact that it is God who is foreseeing things which are future in relation to us. When human beings have foreknowledge, such problems with free will are not considered. Suppose two individuals, A and B, who know one another well, where A tries to mislead B about what he is going to do, and B sees through the deception, and foresees what A is really going to do. In this case, anyone can see that there is no way in which B's foreknowledge can take anything from A's freedom in doing it, and this property of foreknowledge is the same, whether it is possessed by man or by God. Omniscience does not change the meaning and nature of knowledge, any more than the status of a created being can prevent the freedom of the will.

10. *The Free Choice of the Will*, bk 3, chap. 3, [8].

5

Self and Initiation: Conflicting Ideas

Introductory

This chapter is concerned with some characteristically Guénonian ideas, centered on what is said in his *Initiation and Spiritual Realization*.[1] These ideas include a number of obscure realities which play an important part in Guénon's works as a whole and in the ways in which we conceive personal identity. They are used in ways which are different from normal usage, and include Realization, Supra-formal states, Tradition, Initiation, and Identification. Those who empathize with the transcendental and objective importance assigned to these things should note that no attempt is ever made to define any of them, or to indicate any means of verifying them. Those who want to understand them must therefore understand and believe in them without the help of the usual academic methods and concrete examples.

One difficulty of discussing Guénon's thought is that it is informed with a lively religious sentiment which is combined with ideas which, in full rigor, would seem to exclude it. On the strictly conceptual level, therefore, we should have to think in ways quite different from the usual mental processes in order to follow the above ideas.

Where verification is concerned, for example, people no doubt visited Guénon, who would have introduced some of them to various

1. René Guénon, *Initiation and Spiritual Realization* (Hillsdale, NY: Sophia Perennis, 2001).

individuals who were credited with being able to confer initiations. Similarly, we need not doubt that some of those thus introduced received various kinds of instruction and ritual ministrations from these persons. Should that not verify the main idea here? In fact, this is not at all clear.

Suppose these initiatory encounters had taken place *before* those involved had read what Guénon had written about initiation. Would they then be saying the same things about these initiations that Guénon was saying? For that to be possible, these things would have to have so clearly objective a nature that all who encountered them must have said more or less the same things about them. But in that case, the number of others who testified of them in the same way as Guénon would by now be very great with the passage of the centuries. As things are, Guénon stands practically alone in his treatment of this subject.

Besides, to know what the key ideas really mean, one must also know what they are *not*, i.e., things that only resemble them, and this is why it is frustrating that we are not given any information about the sources from whence they are derived. Neither can we tell how much is owing to Guénon himself. What is clear is that there are certain words which are always used with a special intention, which is that of transforming the reader's point of view. For some, this can break up the ideas of reality and normality which we unwittingly acquire from modern education and conditions of employment, and open the mind to a spiritual reality, when the usual forms of instruction have failed to do so.

There is an undeniable charismatic power in these ideas, but that is not a guarantee of theoretical correctness. The ideas of Realization, Tradition, Identification, and Initiation are, nominally speaking, all taken from either secular culture or orthodox religion, but are now given a new dimension of meaning which was not that of the official teachers of the traditional faiths. Nevertheless, Guénon's claim to speak on behalf of the traditional religions is made with total conviction, even though he does not quote any of their living representatives.

For many people, his writings broke the hypnotic spell of history, which was their spiritual prison. Up to Guénon's time, most of the educated felt unable to think outside the historical progression of thought into which they were born. For those so affected, it was a revelation to see that they could equally well identify with the wisdom of antiquity without dependence on the derivative and ever-deviating culture which had succeeded it. The ideas developed by Guénon are based on a conviction of the truth of a monistic mysticism as taught by Shankara. This position was not felt to be challenged by the ideas of Fabre D'Olivet, whom Guénon also regarded as an authority on the esoteric, even though he says:

> Every time that one has claimed to found the Universe upon the existence of a sole material or spiritual nature, and to make proceed from this sole nature the explanation of all phenomena, one has become exposed and always will be, to insurmountable difficulties. It is always in asking what the origin of Good and Evil is, that all systems of this sort have been irresistibly overthrown, from Moschus, Leucippus, and Epicurus, down to Spinoza and Leibniz . . . .[2]

Guénon's commitment to the monistic element of Hinduism was not moderated either by his conviction that all traditions were equally sources of truth, together with the fact that this doctrine does not appear in the other traditions.

It should be borne in mind that the apparently central subjects here, such as initiation and supra-formal states, are worthy of consideration not so much for their own sake as an answer to a pressing practical issue which is not directly referred to as such, namely, the true purpose of traditional religion. Is it to lead and teach from immutable principles, or is it to give rubber stamp approval on God's behalf to contemporary culture? This most of all concerns the select few who are not mentally products of their own time, for whom Guénon was writing, and who feel the spiritual crisis of modern times most deeply.

2. *The Golden Verses of Pythagoras*, §7, p155, Nayan Louise Redfield, tr. (Montana: Kessinger Publishing, 1992).

Self and Initiation: Conflicting Ideas

Intellect and Mental States

In the Foreword to this book, Jean Reyor brings to the fore an essential Guénonian subject, the 'edenic state,' and the possibility of recovering it through initiation. From an orthodox point of view, this is one of the most questionable ideas in Guénon's writings, even though it may superficially appear orthodox. Many Christians are likely to find it acceptable because baptism removes Original Sin. But this is not the same as saying that the Fall can be reversed *in itself.* Judaism, Christianity, and Islam are based on the conviction that the Fall can only be reversed from without, that is, by moving forwards to a revealed way of salvation which is in any case ultimately superior to the 'edenic state'. To deny this is to take away the basic purpose of orthodox religion, just as much as do humanistic denials of the reality of sin.

If it was so possible to reverse 'time's arrow' in this sphere, history would be too trivialized to have any meaning. Besides, if we *could* make the edenic state happen again, the Fall would have to happen again as well. Such an idea could only be confused with regeneration by baptism where orthodox beliefs are weak or half-forgotten. In reality the restoration to grace after individual sin does not mean that one ceases to be the person who sinned, and similarly, the removal of Original Sin by baptism cannot make anyone into a person who was never fallen.

However, the idea of recovering the 'edenic state' has an important effect on one's religious position: if it is accepted, the claims of orthodox religion are now restricted in a way which would make it purely exoteric. Orthodox religion, however necessary in other ways, could now be seen to lie within bounds set by some larger reality, i.e., the world of initiation, to which we are being given the key. Orthodoxy is at once made more important in one way, while being reduced in another.

Despite appearances, therefore, there is no unequivocal advocacy of orthodox religion to be found here. Guénon's premise, made clear in a number of places, that the great majority of mankind is incurably ignorant and stupid is applied to the religiously orthodox nearly as much as to those who are not. This is a position which he shares with other schools of thought including those of Existentialism and followers of Gurdjieff, whom he would not have made a common cause with.

Guénon denies that 'pure and transcendent intellectual knowledge' has anything mental or human about it, in a way which reveals what a materialistic idea he has of the human state. He is uncomfortably close to the idea that human beings are just a more sophisticated kind of animal which, if true, would allow them no basis for wanting to be anything else. Obviously, knowledge could not be human by origin if human nature comprised nothing supra-individual, but what evidence is there for that? Even if it was not human by origin, it would still have to merge with the mental level if anyone is to know that he knows it, or even know anything about it. The knowledge in question is referred to as 'effective,' though no indication is given as to how or why it is effective, or for what purposes.

Similarly, he contrasts it with forms of thought which 'achieve no effective results,' but here again he gives no indication of what an effective result might be, nor how we could identify it if we encountered it. Such statements cannot be argued with, but that is no guarantee of their truth. In the same chapter, 'Metaphysics and Dialectic', true to his reductionist views about the individual, Guénon asserts that it is impossible for the individual to rediscover his source, because he 'obviously cannot surpass himself by his own means,' as though it were self-evident. This, however, is just what Plotinus thought the individual *could* do, since Neoplatonic man was understood to be an epitome of all levels of being. All that was specifically individual about him was united to supra-individual realities in the same person. Should we exclude Plotinus from traditional wisdom?

To deny man's inherent spirituality is to adopt an idea of the person which would make our possession of metaphysical knowledge inexplicable. But in reality, the presence of such knowledge, inherent in mankind, is one of the essentials of traditionalism, with its semi-independence of historically-determined authority. Schuon has many times endorsed this with the idea that the intellect belongs to both the natural and the supernatural at once. Where Guénon seems to set this aside, it is probably for the purpose of challenging the false equilibrium of human nature, but in this case we drift away from theory into practical matters. However, the practical need for a positive change of life does not in any case mean that our natural state is limited of itself. One could only see it that way by taking a common sense view of the self as though it were an eternal truth, and not as the arrangement of subjectivity which it really is. As such, it should not determine discussions of the esoteric.

Salvation and Initiation

An idea of salvation is given which consists in a liberation from the conditions of manifested beings. What, in this case would be saved? The intellect? But that does not need salvation. The ego, as Guénon calls the soul, can only be saved or 'liberated' by dissolving the illusion that it is separate from the 'Self'. But this is of no conceivable concern to the ego. If it must cease to exist, why should the exact means of its termination be of any interest to anyone? To people without religious beliefs, it always seems obvious that the soul or 'ego' ceases to exist, but their point of view is the last one to receive consideration here.

When speaking of 'effective initiation,' and the distinction between it and 'virtual initiation', these things are expressed as though the whole nature of what was involved in them lay in the ritual actions themselves, and as though nothing was contributed either by God or by the persons initiated. (God is never referred to throughout this book). This is what one would expect of magic, not religion. And yet, the initiation, of whatever kind it may be, cannot be independent in this way, since it is obviously a relational entity. While the initiate, the act of initiation, and the reality into which he is initiated are separable for abstract thought, this does not mean that they can be similarly separable in objective fact. Yet Guénon ignores this, as he ignores the fact that the distinction between the consciousness of the soul and the content of that consciousness also exists only for thought.

If we allow for the interactions that must exist in all initiatic relations, and the differences owing to different individualities, what would be an 'effective' initiation for one person would be a 'virtual' one for another, and vice-versa. In the case of the 'effective' kind, we must assume that it gives rise to enough faith to change the initiate's values and way of living. But where Guénon does say what he means by an initiation, he only says that it is 'the initial transmission of a spiritual influence.' This is so vague an idea, that innumerable things could fulfil this role, including a religious painting, or a conversation with a devout person, hearing a sermon, or looking at Gothic or Islamic architecture. If we believe in a personal God, and in the reality of other persons, the transmission of a spiritual influence is perfectly intelligible, but if there was only an impersonal 'Principle' and an unreal 'ego', from whom or from what, and to whom or to what, does the influence go, and what purpose could it have?

Guénon proceeds to speak of the preparation which is necessary prior to 'realization,' without saying what must be understood by this word. There is obviously such a thing as self-realization, in a sense where it implies the full development of all one's best potentialities. But this is something which can be verified by observation, and nothing so tangible is meant here. He implies that it must be more than something theoretical, however, but the practical application of 'realization' is never specified. It could not apply to the Principle, which is by definition real enough, whereas everything else that could be named is not real at all.

This implies an idea of God which is non-personal and completely passive in relation to nature, since all action in this book is ascribed to human beings alone. Initiation, therefore, can only come to us from other people. Jacob Boehme's encounter with the stranger in the shop is *a priori* an initiation for Guénon, because the only alternative would be that initiation was not always necessary. Here we can see the intrusion of ideology, since the conclusion—the unconditional necessity for initiation—dictates the way in which one interprets things which may or may not lead us to it.

'Spiritual influences' are referred to further on, but again with no more explanation as to what this might mean. In this connection, an idea of prayer is expressed which resembles that of Plotinus, but which is far from what is believed about it by religious orthodoxy. For Guénon, it only means that 'a collectivity can use the subtle force at its disposal,' into which a spiritual influence may or may not intervene. He says clearly that prayer 'addresses itself most immediately *to the collective entity*' (my italics), and that only through the latter does it contact, not God, but 'a spiritual influence'.

The doctrinal position behind this is clear enough. It expresses the idea that the individual is fixed immovably in his place in the Great Chain of Being, which spiritually encloses him on all sides. Any spiritual help he gets, therefore, must come either from others in the same state, or from those in the next higher state. This fixed position in the Chain of Being is taken to rule out any kind of direct relation to God, even though this relation is the presupposition of all traditional religions. The reason why such an extreme conclusion is drawn is clear enough: only on this basis can initiation be absolutely necessary, if one is to move any closer to God or the Principle.

It is not really a contradiction to say that all beings have places in the Great Chain of Being, while they are also able to relate directly to God, since God alone is not bound by the limitations of created beings. This relation is made actual by means of grace revealed by God in the universal religions. The last point is vital, since the above idea could well be true in a world where there had never been any revelation from God, but to prescind from revelation and grace like this is a strange procedure for a work on spirituality. Christian tradition has always accepted both the inclusion of the person in the Chain of Being and that of direct access to God, as one would expect from its inclusive tendency. In this regard, Guénon gives to religious orthodoxy with one hand and takes away with the other, rousing a spiritual desire and a sense of spiritual imprisonment at the same time.

Though he speaks of initiatic organizations, none is ever named. He even mentions 'the supreme spiritual center', though we are not told whether this is Mecca, the Vatican, Lhasa, or somewhere even more superior and quite hidden. The various traditions have their centers, of course, but to assert *a priori* that there is a supreme center is to beg the question as to whether all the religions are so many different offshoots of one universal tradition. The approach used in this connection is always to allude to this unity as though it were something whose reality was so obviously real that nothing more need be said about it, which is certainly effective psychologically.

True to his low estimate of modern civilization, Guénon claims that the majority of those who offer initiations are imposters, whether they are consciously so or not. Those of them who are in good faith are possibly the more dangerous, since they combine sincerity with untruth. This raises major practical problems for those who want to receive what is meant here by initiation. How are the true ones to be distinguished from the false? Guénon will only say that the true ones are 'effective', as though this word could make anything clear. There can be few things which have no effect at all, but to be specific about the actual effects of initiation would make it possible to check these statements by experience. This, however, is not attempted here, or even considered.

Tradition and Culture

A further topic is that of 'a wholly profane existence,' this being one from which all traditional elements are excluded. It is not clear whether such a thing is possible, since most of secular culture is more or less indirectly derived from tradition, besides being unconsciously affected by the traditional religions within it. Guénon makes a commonplace observation that people in the modern world practice their religions in a way that has no contact with the rest of their lives, and so apparently cannot affect them. Although this is stated as though it were obvious, it is in fact not at all obvious that religious practices have no contact with the rest of a person's life just because that contact is not conscious or deliberate. As long as the person forms a unity at all, and is not in a schizoid condition, the activities of one part of his or her life must have their effects on the other parts, provided only that this influence is not deliberately resisted.

For this reason, it is possible, given some sincerity, that religion in one part of a life can subtly transform the whole life in a way which is natural and spiritual at once. Guénon's criticism of modern culture is in this instance an over-valuation of consciousness which he usually does not allow elsewhere, as where he speaks of the passive and perfunctory participation which traditional civilizations invite, as though it were a merit, and conscious commitment did not matter. In other words, what he presents as a merit in the life in a traditional culture must also extend to modern cultures where religious practice does not visibly affect much else. This conclusion would also be reasonable, in view of the fact that the idea of observances simply having no effect is only a popular notion, because, metaphysically understood, every action must necessarily have an effect, as Guénon understood better than anyone.

The criticism levelled at modern culture here is based on an assumption that there is an absolute divide between the world of the spirit and the natural world. That the latter could be naturally permeated by the former hardly appears to be thought of, even though we are not taken as far as a formal dualism. What is also strange about this position is that traditionalist thought in general is heavily dependent on the idea of what Schuon calls the 'naturally supernatural', the inherent spirituality of man, that is, his 'theomorphism'.

On what other basis can we rate the traditional role of the intellect so highly? Guénon no doubt believes in it, but believes at the same time, like Augustine, that mankind is but a *massa damnosa* with no operative intellect. It could be replied that this inherent spirituality still has to be awakened before it can be actual, but this does not give us the right to assume that this awakening is not happening anywhere, just because we cannot see it happening under conditions which we recognize and understand.

It is pointed out that different people can spend their lives acting in much the same ways, while having points of view which have almost nothing in common. To some minds, that might cause scepticism as to the importance of such different points of view, if the 'bottom line' must always be the same. Nevertheless, Guénon criticizes those who think that human life is always the same, even though he regards the individual state as unreal in any case. In connection with human motivation, he claims that morality does not have the meaning it has for us in civilizations which are 'completely different' from our own 'in every respect'.

If in fact civilizations could differ *toto caelo* like this, the human state would have to have so vast a range of possibilities that there could be no reason to pursue any one of them rather than another, but does that tally with what we know about ourselves? We know that the same universal values are respected everywhere, but a completely different civilization could well relegate the Good, the True, and the Beautiful to the lowest place among its priorities. In reality, civilizations only differ completely in externals, for example, in the way that black is worn for mourning in the West and white in the Far East, whereas no civilization ever thinks that one can dispose of the dead without mourning.

But if Guénon was right, there would be such civilizations, and the springs of human motivation would differ too widely for it to be possible to classify all concerned as human beings. But the necessity for productive labor, defense of territory, and the raising of children leaves too little room for such deviations, and in fact all the available evidence shows that qualities of moral goodness, intellectual power and vision, and physical and artistic beauty rule in all civilizations, which produce endless adaptations and rearrangements of them.

According to Guénon's idea of tradition, morality is replaced in other civilizations by a ritual conformity to certain archetypal patterns. This is supposed to be spiritually superior to the moral perspective, which is taken to be a kind of degeneration from the ritual position. Moral conscience, he says, 'requires no intellectual comprehension,' though in fact it must always require some intellectual intuition of good and evil. He does not relate this to the traditionalist position that people can just as well participate in a traditional civilization without comprehending it, simply by its regulation of their normal activities.

If it were true that the moral perspective was inferior to the ritual, the revelation of the Ten Commandments could by no means be what it is for religious orthodoxy. There was however, a strong moral code in ancient Egypt, alongside its ritual practices, which endured for long ages, so there seems to be no need to have the one rather than the other. In fact, moral values are universal, whereas ritual practices vary endlessly. The belief that our moral rights and wrongs also have meaning in relation to God is also universal, which should rule out the idea that they are merely human social regulations, as Guénon evidently believes.

In 'The Glorification of Work', Guénon says some very perceptive things about the role of work in the context of self-realization, no matter how that is understood. Here are ideas of universal significance, crossing the boundaries of religious belief in an intelligible manner. In regard to 'The Sacred and the Profane', Guénon makes it a merit of traditional civilizations that they organize life in such a way that participation in the tradition by everyone is ensured by most everyday activities, regardless of their ostensible purpose. Nevertheless, there would have to be a personal commitment to some part of this culture at least, or else this kind of participation would be purely superficial.

It may be that people can be educated in a subliminal manner by the symbolism of a traditional culture, and that is no doubt part of its purpose, but this is something very hard to verify. If it did have this effect, a traditional culture which lasted for some centuries would have the effect of making its inhabitants progressively more and more spiritual. The same lessons would be applied to successive generations until a very great spiritual momentum was built up. In this case, the Renaissance would have to be viewed in a spiritually much more positive way than Guénon and other Perennialists would allow, and the eager adoption of Platonism when it became accessible in the fifteenth century would have to be seen as a fruition of traditional wisdom.

In reality, human minds are extremely difficult to influence for any purpose, regardless of their intelligence and talents. This is because each soul is born with a specific nature, which largely dictates the kinds of experience which it will seek and assimilate. Only in borderline cases can deliberately-applied influences have any effect. Not only does this mean that the effective influence of traditional culture is a lot less than one might expect, it also means that the effects on people of an avowedly profane culture are a lot less as well, as the failure of Communism indicates.

However, if each person is effectively a monad, developing itself according to an internal principle, this still does not explain why there are ages when many are open to spiritual wisdom, and ages when very few are. Some additional principle must be reckoned with, one which causes a progressive reduction in the spiritual potentialities with which souls come to birth over long periods of time, or causes the birth of greater numbers of those with few or no such possibilities. This is where one can see the action of a cyclic law, tending relentlessly from Quality to Quantity.

Where the idea of influence is concerned, Guénon's use of the expression 'effective influence' is not much amplified, and it appears that he is only thinking of external and visible means of regulation which could involve a pre-emptive action on man's freedom to choose between God and the world. In such cases, one must believe that external pressures will give rise to a positive interior response. While this certainly happens with some people, many others do not so respond, but remain open to alternatives which are spiritually dubious. This is why theocracies inevitably fail as the number of those born without spiritual potential increases with the descending cyclic process. There is evidently a contradiction here: from a vision of the liberating power of pure intellect, we thus end up with the idea of theocracy, where one socially conforms and imitates other people. Plato went through a similar *volte-face* by the time he wrote his *Laws*, so this may well be a contradiction in the human condition itself. The inner conflict here is common to traditionalists in general: an intellectual assertiveness, combined with a desire to be subject to social direction and support.

Guénon's belief that the sacred and the profane should not be allowed to exist in separate realms shows that he considers theocracy to be the only valid option. In this connection, he states that members of the clergy who perform a role, or 'intervene', in the secular world can only do so on the basis that this realm is legitimate in itself. Since their vocation is the sacred, their behavior must therefore be irrational, even contradictory, and their thinking, he says, does not differ from that of their adversaries.

This kind of thinking is applicable to present-day society in view of worsening spiritual conditions. As the cyclic movement draws mankind further from its collective relations to spiritual reality, it must require ever greater concessions to its materialized state from anyone who wishes to interact with it. From this, it would follow that a cut-off point must be reached, at which the concessions required will outweigh any spiritual good that could be achieved by them. This was what Guénon believed to have already happened in the twentieth century, though here he is clearly in conflict with those who believe that the saving message is independent of all human conditions. There is the problem with this, however, that a message which is relevant for absolutely any culture must somehow remain unmodified by its relations to the alien values around it. In reality, there is in fact a degree of corruption and deviation with which one cannot hold dialogue without conferring legitimacy on it, however little that is intended. Beyond this point, religion gets equated with the public activities that were meant to manifest it, and is thus evacuated of content. The Gospel warning of the approaching darkness: 'Night comes when no one can work' (John 9:4), has relevance to extreme cyclic conditions, as well as to the approach of the Passion in the literal sense of the text.

Salvation or Deliverance?

In the chapter on 'Salvation and Deliverance', the orthodox belief in salvation is presented as being necessarily inferior to the undefined 'deliverance,' as is usually done by the Perennialists. But how is this known, unless one has actually died, and experienced these things at first-hand? Otherwise, it may only be a matter of words. If the disparagements of salvation made by Perennialists were examined by a visitor from another planet, he would most probably think that salvation was a physical object, like a garment which had been tried on and been found to be too small. He would never guess that it was in fact a transcendental and atemporal reality, unknown to anyone still alive.

Orthodox theology allows the idea of different degrees or levels of salvation, as must be well known to anyone with any knowledge of tradition, although this is hardly ever referred to by those who teach that salvation is something *per se* inadequate, and must be replaced with something beyond definition. The individual state is always equated with a *limited* individual state, as where he says that the great majority are incapable of going beyond 'the limits of the individual state,' as though there was but one standard individual condition.

The Platonists never saw the individual state as limited as such, because they found nothing in it to prevent its limits from being extended indefinitely. A modern Christian Platonist makes this point as follows:

> The mind expands *pari passu* with the things it perceives and knows. The soul... is in a sense [not in the mentalist sense] the creator of the world. Degrees of reality mean mainly degrees in the apprehension of reality as a kingdom of values; and these values are not merely exhibited to the soul as something outside and alien to itself; they are, and increasingly become, the life of the soul, which, as it ascends to the spiritual world, finds the absolute values less and less external to itself.[3]

Given this idea of reality, the Guénonian ideas of initiation and de-individuation can look like a passion for forcing doors which were never locked. The life of Christ was the life of an individual, as were the lives of the founders of the other religions. If any given individual is limited, therefore, that is either through his immaturity or his own fault. Different orders of individuality would imply similar differences of salvation, but instead of acknowledging different levels of salvation, Guénon speaks of 'an effective realization of a supra-individual though still conditioned state, not to mention Deliverance.'

The terms involved here are well known, simply because the conceptions of 'effective', 'realization', and 'supra-formal', are all normal mental operations. But although these concepts are universal, we cannot assume that they must remain meaningful even outside the experiences to which they belong. In fact, Guénon never says whether he is summarizing experiences, or simply expressing a theory. It is true that, as theoretical ideas, supra-individual states can also be known as higher developments of our own state, but this not only does not support monistic conclusions, but rather opposes them, since higher extensions of our being must make it less needful to escape from it.

For man, salvation or deliverance must be events in the biography of the same individual if they are to happen at all; without that condition, one could not claim that anything had happened. But Guénon firmly rejects the belief that anyone could learn or

3. W.R. Inge, *God and the Astronomers*, pp 47–48 (London: Longmans, Green & Co., 1933).

understand any more in the hereafter than they have done in this world, although many or most of those who believe in eternal life suppose that this should be one of its main purposes. His reason for this is not hard to see, however, because if the soul could progress in the hereafter, there would be no reason for the downgrading of salvation as such. But in this context we are committed to the spiritual impotence of the individual soul and the consequent absolute necessity for initiation as the way out of it. On this basis, progress in the hereafter must be excluded. If this exclusion is accepted, along with its implicit denial of any access to God in this life, the result will be either despair or a passionate commitment to initiation.

Although salvation is a *pis aller*, it is affirmed that most men cannot attain a supra-individual state. But how do we understand those individuals who can pass into such states? Does it mean that the supra-individual state now *contains* those individuals? By no means. If it did, it would no longer be supra-individual. But the only alternative to this would be that no one has really 'passed' or 'gone' anywhere. In this case, we would be using a language suited to the idea of persons 'going to Heaven' in order to say that man's true immortality is a state which knows no more of him than the science of biology knows of one particular animal.

Guénon mentions man's 'ultimate destination', which is neither God nor Heaven, because he avoids God by separating the Beyond-Being of the Principle from the Being of the personal God, who is thereby made into a mere personification of the Principle. No reason is given here or elsewhere as to why these must be two separate realities, apart from the implicit reason that the goal of Identification could only be conceivable with the most abstract or indeterminate conception of God in isolation from any other. This idea of the divine is one which was adopted by Schuon as well. His writings make it easier to see how the Theistic idea of God is effectively deconstructed in this form of doctrine:

> [In] short, it (*Maya*, illusion) encompasses the Creator as well as the creature, 'God' as well as the 'world'; only the 'pure Absolute',

'Beyond-Being', *Parabrahma* or *Atma*, escapes its grasp.... *Maya* determines God, the creative person....[4]

In this kind of thinking, the idea of God is emptied of what would make it truly God-like, since it is divided out among different concepts, i.e., 'pure Absolute', 'Beyond-Being', 'Creative Person', *Maya*. No proof is offered for this, because the idea that God-as-Absolute and God-as-Relative are separate realities is clearly unverifiable, and a similar remark applies to Being and Beyond-Being. It is noteworthy that this conception does not in any case really get us any further away from anthropomorphism, because the idea that these two aspects of divinity must be separate in fact, because they are so for human thought, commits us to a belief that Divinity follows the properties of human thought. The more commonplace representations of God, where they are formed by images that impress the imagination, are safer, as not liable to be taken literally.

Whether one believes in this or not, one thing is clear, namely that this is above all else a system, despite Guénon's disavowal of systems. Guénon claims that when mystics speak of union with God, they cannot mean Yoga because they are 'only' concerned with salvation. Their union could only be an 'exterior' or 'relative' union if their individuality still existed, though it is not explained what the union could mean if the individuality did cease to exist. He then claims that the mystics had never conceived of the 'Supreme Identity', when in fact it was well known in the Middle Ages as the heresy of the Beghards or the Free Spirit. The mystics of those times, including Ruysbroek and Eckhart, knew of it and dissociated themselves from it. The idea of the 'Supreme Identity' is an example of an idea which can be two different things, one of them a platitude, in this case that God is indeed God, and the other, that there is nothing but God.

Where Guénon states that the Beatific Vision of orthodox religion is separated from 'Deliverance' (meaning God?) 'by the entire extent of the angelic worlds,' he shows as clearly as possible his

4. *Survey of Metaphysics and Esoterism*, p55. (Bloomington: World Wisdom Books, 2000).

belief that one's place in the Great Chain of Being must block all access to God. If this were true, one would have to deny to man the 'divine spark' or *synteresis* in the soul which is the key to that access and regard God as confined by the limitations of particular beings. But this is the last thing that an esotericist could wish to deny, because without it we should be as enclosed by our mortality as completely as are the animals. If this were the intention, it would be hard to see why the Guénonians should reject Darwinism so completely. Without the 'divine spark', there could be no metaphysical knowledge, and therefore no esoteric. This contradiction could only arise in minds where the human state is dogmatically identified with everything most mortal and trivial about it.

Denial of Individuality

Both the giving and the seeking of esoteric wisdom are often associated with intellectual pride, to which a chapter is devoted here. Guénon objects to this expression that it is self-contradictory, since intellectuality is supra-individual, while pride is solely a condition of the individual as such. This argument involves the assumption already observed, that the individual person is essentially one-dimensional, and cannot comprise any other nature, any more than can an individual stone. The traditional idea that each individual soul has its own system of all the supra-individual Forms or archetypes is inconvenient for the initiatic idea of tradition, and so is ignored. If it were taken into account, it would allow the idea that an individual could become proud because of powers which were supra-formal, just as easily as of powers which were purely individual.

Once it is allowed that the personality remains a unity, however diverse its powers, this self-unity ensures that our lower nature is free to react in any way it likes to the higher nature, unless it is disciplined. On this basis, 'intellectual pride' is a realistic expression. Not only is there such a condition, it is by no means confined to those who have developed their intellect beyond the average, since it also occurs in those who want to deny an intellectuality they do not share. In this inverted, and equally widespread form, one makes one's own intellect a standard for others, whether it deserves to be or not. Here is precisely where pride intervenes, with its inevitable preference-for-self, even though it is as much at home with unintelligence as with intelligence. In its inverted form, it is a means used by the majority, not quite unconsciously, to prevent people from moving out of the herd, when they might otherwise find the courage to rise above its level. Guénon has shown elsewhere that the prevailing cosmic condition functions as though designed to retain those who once enter it.

From the above, he proceeds to another argument which is not effective, because it betrays an ignorance of psychology. It is claimed that there cannot be any such thing as intellectual pride, because intellectuality reveals the individuality to be 'strictly null' in relation to the Principle. Whether the latter point is true or not, the belief that one is nothing very often has a perverse appeal for the egoistic, and makes them feel more important than ever. Human irrationality is endless, and it allows intellectual pride in this case because some people will identify with the Principle in relation to which they are supposedly nothing. If this attitude is not entirely foolish, it is precisely because the soul with its intellectual faculty is the cause of one's individuation, though this cannot be seen by those who see no connection between their intellect and their own persons. There are no boundaries between the soul of the individual and the truths he or she knows, and this means that the way in which we know non-empirical truths, like that of the Principle which makes everything else insignificant in comparison, depends on our having something in our own souls which corresponds to it.

As the self is a microcosm, there will be nothing 'out there', not even the Principle, which is not in some sense 'in here'. This is not compatible with being nothing. In this case, our 'nothingness' is more truly the relative nothingness of one order of being in relation to another. This rules out both a simplistic reduction of the individual to nullity and the argument that this must exclude intellectual pride. Given the idea that the human individual is an epitome of the real in which formal and supra-formal realities coexist, individual pride and a belief in individual nullity can coexist there as well.

The major problem with pride, which Guénon indicates, is the way in which it inverts the true order of things: according to this order, man must be Yin in relation to the Principle and Yang in relation to the phenomenal world, and thus bring the light of the higher world into the lower one. When pride inverts this, man is Yang in relation to the Principle and Yin in relation to his world and his culture, putting him out of due relation to God and the world at the same time. The universality of pride today can thus be seen in the receptiveness and submissiveness of people to everything and anything *except* God.

While the individuality is in some sense a nullity according to traditional principles, as Guénon says, it cannot be so without qualification. While its own peculiarities have no meaning in relation to first principles, its status simply as a knowing subject is essential if the doctrines are to be part of the world of consciousness. The latter relation is necessary if doctrines are to become actual and not merely potential, and for that they require the energy of consciousness which individual beings provide. The fact that Guénon does not allow for this could easily be owing to his adherence to a well-known or rather notorious Scholastic adage that individuation is caused only by matter, and not by the Forms instantiated in it.

If this were true, there could be no individual souls or intellects, as Averroes thought. However, this idea is false because it attributes to matter, or the material principle, a causal power of its own, when in fact it is by definition purely passive. It is in fact the Forms which individuate their instantiations, as well as causing their qualities. To attribute a separate causal power to matter is in fact to confuse it with *material objects*, in which Forms are already active. Because of this confusion, Scholastics departed from traditional metaphysics, and prepared the way for scientific materialism. Where 'individual' is taken to mean 'mere matter' the philosophical consequences can only undermine the idea of the soul as a 'subsistent form,' and create an idea of the person supported by neither Plato nor Aristotle, nor by traditional wisdom as a whole.

Supra-Formal States

The expression 'supra-formal states' is often used here, though it is so little used by other authors, except those following Guénon, that it is hard to be sure what it means. A 'state' is by definition a condition relative to certain other conditions, particularly those of time and space. Clearly, it cannot exist in this manner without having a definite form, in the ordinary sense of the word, whence a supra-formal state would appear to be contradictory, unless it is integrated with other states which are formal. And yet it is by reason of the supposedly superior reality of supra-formal states that the soul, which is the normal object of salvation, is made to seem hardly worth saving.

It looks as though the reasoning here is that something which clearly needed salvation did not merit salvation, simply because of being in need of it. In this case, salvation would be reserved for what was beyond change. The role of the supra-formal element occurs in connection with direct and reflected contemplation, because a Form, 'before' instantiation is in some, but not all, respects supra-formal. Where he speaks of the essential difference between 'metaphysical or initiatic realization' and the less-esteemed 'mystical realization', we are not told whether this is known to be a matter of experience, or whether this is simply a matter of the definitions of terms.

As before, we must consider whether this distinction is intrinsic to the things in question, or whether it arises because of the different types of person who experience them. The key to the difference between the two kinds of realization is said to lie in two different types of contemplation, the 'direct' and the 'reflected'. From what is said about the above, it is clear that the 'direct' kind concerns the realities as they are in themselves, that is, the Forms, while the 'reflected' kind concerns realities 'in their reflection in the individual domain,' that is, the instantiations of the Forms. The Forms are in some respects supra-individual, but for all that, they belong to the intelligence of individual persons.

Nevertheless, the supra-formal reality is not an object, standing over against the subject, divided from it by a sharp line, because in reality the two flow freely into one another, as Plotinus taught. Against this, however, we are presented with the conception that 'mysticism never implies an identification,' on the grounds that it retains the distinction of subject and object, the two being presumed to have no mutual infusion, but remaining juxtaposed like material objects. He has already affirmed that knowledge necessarily involves an 'identification', and on this basis, the mystics could not be said to know God.

Although nothing as extreme as this is actually said, it would follow from what is said here. Besides, it does not appear exactly what is being identified with what. If it is the initiate himself who becomes identified with the Principle, while he continues to live, this would imply that the Principle must become identified with the initiate at the same time, if identity means what it says. But since the Principle is thought of here as entirely non-formal, such an identification with a formal being must be impossible.

However, if we say that it is not the whole person, but the supra-individual part of his soul which becomes consciously identified with the Principle, there would be no such problem. This would be an orthodox position which is common to many forms of spirituality, but in this case it obviously could not support claims for superiority over orthodox beliefs.

In 'Doctrine and Method', we return to the idea of there being many different ways, all of which lead to the same final state. Unlike the points of departure, the final point of arrival is always the same, although this is a determinate relation, which implies some element of form. In this case, the differences between all traditional religions could only be so many modes of expression, needed to bring the same truth to diverse peoples and cultures. This is to ignore the fact that there are religious traditions which do not come from God except inasmuch as everything does, but which can all nevertheless make the same claim for inclusion. Besides, some of the traditions will be more adequate revelations than others, while yet others will be worthless or evil.

Guénon says that traditional truth cannot take the form of a system, because the specific form of a system results only from what it excludes. This is surely true, in view of the endless complexity of traditional and post-traditional cultures, but although this truth is recognized in the abstract, Guénon had no wish to be guided by it. His method is precisely to reduce all traditional religions to a single system, and that follows from his main purpose, that of finding the same truth in all of them.

Conversely, without an overriding system, the traditions could easily seem to contradict one another, but with a system, one is putting the truth on a Procrustean bed. The system adopted here is in any case notable for a simplicity which is too bare and abstract to represent the full range of man's potentialities. It is one which invites comparison with the abstract theories of scientists. In accordance with the same set of ideas, he refers in chapter 30 to the Vedantist idea that the individual embodied soul or *jivatma* is separate from *Atma* only by an illusion. In other words, there could be only one reality which was not an illusion. Despite the monistic intention here, the result is an irreducible dualism between the Real and the illusory, because the latter is set free to be a kind of 'second God', since it has nothing in common with the Real.

This kind of division between the Real and the illusory is a dichotomy which ignores the complexities of the real world. But that is what results from a system. The passage of the being to a 'supra-individual realization' is expressed metaphorically, as though it were a journey. A passage logically has to refer to someone or something which passes, but this is not what Guénon means. In reality, it is more a matter of one thing disappearing while another one comes into existence, but even this is incorrect because it implies that a change takes place at the supra-formal level in response to one which takes place at the formal level.

Put a little more technically, the question is whether the formal states preceding the realization can form a single temporal sequence with the supra-formal ones which are supposed to follow after it. If they can, the hard distinction between formal and supra-formal fails, and if not, nothing could be said to have converted to anything else. What we should be left with, then, is simply the disappearance of one being while a non-personal reality continues to exist. Some may believe that this has nothing in common with the natural dissolution which materialists suppose to be the end of all beings, but the difference involved is hard to define.

This raises a question as to why people in both East and West are willing to believe that finite or 'formal' beings are essentially unreal. For the great majority of those who think in this way, there is only one reason, namely, that finite beings seldom ever appear to last very long. The impermanence of all natural things strikes the imagination. (Some philosophers would say that finite beings were unreal because their existence is derivative from higher realities, like the Forms. But this would not suffice for the amount of response to illusionism which actually does exist.)

It is easy to see that this negative judgement on formal being depends on the premise that time and temporal experience are completely real, which is a very strange assumption for people who are committed to a metaphysical knowledge for which the true realities are the eternal or atemporal ones. There is a fundamental contradiction here. If the unreality of passing-time as we experience it is affirmed, we thereby lose any basis for denying the reality of the formal or finite beings which appear to us as limited by it, since the fact that they do not appear to last long need not mean anything. Conversely, if the temporal experience of impermanence and decay is a revelation of true reality, the true philosophy could only be Empiricism, and all metaphysical systems must be false, since they place the real in the invisible and the eternal. In short, this kind of Vedantist idea of the esoteric depends on a naive belief in what ordinary sense-perception seems to tell us about ourselves.

Some metaphysical studies of the temporal condition show the appearances and disappearances of things in time to be illusions arising from the limitations of our powers of perception. This is poles apart from saying that these existences are illusory in themselves. Even the fact that existence is by definition dependent and derivative does not prove its unreality, because the causal powers which sustain it are part of the eternal scheme of things.

It is noteworthy that Guénon's system of initiations and supra-formal states was sidelined by Frithjof Schuon, who was the more philosophical of these two men. The best one can say for this system is that it can give one a strong sense of other-worldly reality, and of the insignificance of the things that most people take seriously. But for some people, the benefit of this can be lost when they take these ideas too literally.

Asceticism and Spiritual Action

In 'Ascesis and Asceticism', Guénon refers to a supposed belief that suffering has some value in itself, in a way which shows no understanding of the spiritual meaning it can have. This is as though he knew nothing of the Catholic belief that suffering can be redemptive of both oneself and of others if accepted with faith. In ignoring this, Guénon thinks like a modern intellectual who makes an ideal out of functional perfection, no matter what its purposes. The other objection he raises is that asceticism aims solely at the salvation of the soul, and not 'the effective realization of spiritual states,' as though personal immortality were as limited as some popular images of it, and as though there were not different levels of salvation.

No definition or explanation is given for the idea of 'the effective realization of spiritual states,' nor are we told how this effectiveness could be recognized. Since no traditional authority is quoted in support of this idea, we cannot have any assurance that this is traditional wisdom. Besides, there remains the objection that, if these spiritual states really are states, they must be conditioned, and therefore integrated with other kinds of states; they cannot exist in a vacuum.

At the end of this chapter, the individuality is referred to as 'but a contingency.' In reality, it comprises a range of possibilities from the material to the spiritual, and is the *locus* and basis of consciousness of non-individual realities. To unite oneself 'effectively with the permanent and immutable principle of one's being' (p103, footnote), must be as possible for the individual state as for any other. Otherwise, it would mean that the Principle had a *specifically and purely* non-individual nature, so that it would thus be a determined reality after all.

In connection with the differences between the potentialities of individuals, Guénon claims that inborn wisdom can result from pre-natal conditions in non-human states of existence, from whence it is supposed that we have come. But the occurrence of a rare quality like wisdom is not made any easier to understand by supposing it to be a continuation of the same thing in some other world. Even if this origin were true, it would not explain how it arose in that other world; if it did so by a transfer from a yet more remote world, and so on *ad infinitum*, we should be no nearer an answer. Since wisdom is rare, we would also want to know why there should be so few transmissions of wisdom to this world from others. Does this mean that wisdom is no more common in any of the other worlds than it is in this one? If that were the case, it would be another reason for cosmic pessimism, and would give us no reason for seeking transmigration to other worlds.

In 'Against Quietism', Guénon makes a point against modern activism where he says that activity is 'all the greater and more real as it is exercised in a domain the more remote from that of action.' The point is made that 'non-action' is poles apart from inactivity, because it is free from all the limitations imposed by action in the usual sense of the word. Although he does not say so directly, the power of the non-action of a spiritual state comes from the Law of Cosmic Sympathy, by which any given nature attracts its like and excludes its unlike, by being what it is. The more strongly realized this nature is, the more strong this effect on the world will be.

For this reason, 'non-action' is at its best when deeply concealed. So as to act in the truest sense, the initiate avoids outward distinction from the multitude, while differing profoundly from it inwardly. In this way, his 'action of presence' is not only at its most free, but is safe from outward attack or hindrance.

In regard to high-ranking initiates who take no visible part in the events of the world, this does not mean that they lack goodwill, but that they are so deeply established in the spiritual center of existence that activity on the spiritual periphery (which is what the external world must mean to them) would cause them a deep inner conflict. If they were to act directly on the outside world, 'their exterior would no longer really correspond to their interior,' so their action would be undermined by a certain kind of falsehood. The opposite supposition to this would be that no one could ever identify more than superficially with any state of being, whether spiritual or natural. But this would be a denial of man's higher possibilities, and a claim that mediocrity was universal. The alternatives of pride and humility are not applicable here, because those who identify with the most central state are taking a position outside the personal concerns that could occasion either pride or humility.

Guénon links this to what he calls the higher meaning of anonymity, claiming that it corresponds to a 'liberation' from the individual condition. This can easily be misunderstood, however, because an absence of individuality is more likely to result from a failure of spiritual development, than from spirituality. Better put, it would rather be a development of the individual's extra-individual possibilities. Liberation from the negative aspects of the individual condition must in any case be manifest in consciousness, which is by definition rooted in the individual person. A literal removal of individuality would take the whole thing outside consciousness and therefore beyond all hope of verification.

The final chapter is concerned with those who are invested with a mission. If they do not take on this function by their own choice, there must remain a question as to who or what decides that they shall have it. In Guénon's terms this cannot be God, since he assumes that the highest reality cannot be personal, and it does not appear that the cause is the chance working of natural forces. It may be that such persons exist because of the Principle of Plenitude, which implies a continuity of being, and therefore the existence of mediating forms between all the different kinds. In this case, the mediating entity would be between those who are wholly at one with reality, and those who are wholly at one with unreality, if that is possible. They are separate both from the general class of manifested beings, and from those who have realized the 'Self'. The latter, where they exist in this world, exist in it only in appearance, and can play no direct part in it.

However, if this state is taken to be what orthodox belief understands as Divinity, this inability for direct action would be strange, since the divine must include the power to act directly as well as indirectly. This indicates that the highest state for man is still a specific state, with certain limitations. It may be that Guénon had to ignore this, and take liberties with the normal ideas in order to carry out the mission which he certainly had, and which he has extended to many others.

Conclusions

Despite the theoretical problems raised by Guénon's ideas of initiation, they can open minds to the reality of the spirit where conventional thought does not. For this reason, I would add some observations on the positive effects that come more from the 'tone' of Guénon's thought, than from its literal content. His strange ideas solved various problems involved in showing the spiritual role of the intellect to be a practical reality. Because he was addressing a culture in which the intellect had become simply a tool of the ego, he could only state a case for it in a spiritually truthful manner by driving home its transcendence of the ego by any means possible. Failing this, he would only have worsened the original misconception. For this purpose, the ideas of initiation and supra-formal states are able to make people aware that the intellect has the key to self-transformation, and in a way that strictly philosophical methods do not.

This message was intended for those who were aware of being in the grip of a spiritual crisis, which appeared in the increasing marginalization of the intellect in religious life. Religious leaders tended more and more to have a faith more suited to private individuals, than to those who had to address all intellectual levels. This was a grave departure from tradition, and was making religious faith less accessible to some of those who had more than the usual intelligence and goodwill. From this was born an unheard-of stance, that of doing battle with orthodoxy in the name of orthodoxy. To go on accepting orthodoxy at face value would, in the long term, have meant accepting the complete elimination of the intelligence for anything more than mundane purposes. Since Guénon's time, the world's religious organizations have gone on becoming increasingly instruments of secular political and cultural programmes, and so have begun to militate against what they were first set up for, the salvation of the soul.

If any more justification was required for the traditionalist reversion to principle, it could be found from the fact that society had ceased to be a vehicle for true values, and had consequently ceased to be able to make any moral claims over its own members.

Involuntarily, it had set the individual free to stand apart from it for the sake of truth, and become a focal point for everything the modern world had turned away from. At the same time, the prevailing idea of 'beyond-being' had the effect of separating this option from the reproach of egotism, which is liable to worry those who respect the social morality. The great need to awaken people from a materialistic slumber also meant that Guénon could go to extremes in portraying the modern world as a limbo of the lost, and creating the impression that most modern people were beyond help, by any direct means, at least. This is at least more truthful than the converse idea of progress, and in any case a faith which ignored this issue must end as a mere denial of facts.

However, this still does not take into account Guénon's purpose in making no reference to God, for which I have offered some explanation previously. His writings can only be of interest to those who believe in God, and yet they are the class of reader which will be most offended by this omission.

Guénon adopts this exclusion of God because he is wedded to the belief that the supreme Beyond-being and the supreme Being are objectively separate realities. In other words, he believes that the act of analytical thinking which makes this distinction is a manifestation of an actual separation. But those who see no reason to admit this will see no objection to a personal God at any metaphysical level. In fact, most separations effected by thought do not correspond to physical separations in the outside world. This is an instance where attachment to a theory leads metaphysics to a quite unnecessary clash with orthodoxy.

At the same time, however, he is claiming that beyond the orthodox rites and sacraments, there are higher sacraments, compared with which the latter are mere types and shadows. This bears a curious resemblance to the claims Saint Paul makes for Christianity in comparison with Judaism, though Guénon does not claim to be revealing a new religion, but rather an access to a source of wisdom for those who can combine faith in a tradition with an intellectual independence of it. It may be that these superior rites are a metaphor for what is best and truest in the orthodox ones.

It is as though he reached the idea of a metaphysical self-denial which was designed to upstage and outdo anything that could be required of us by even the most demanding orthodox religion. On that basis, he had a position from whence he could square the circle, so to speak, by being able to affirm the religions absolutely and without reservation from a position to which they had no access or on which they did not operate. This would be acceptable if there were no limit to the degree of self-denial that could be required of us, and that the further we went with it, the better we were. In reality, self-denial is a relativity which, when made absolute, destroys its own meaning and function, whence the paradoxes I have discussed previously. However, it must be said that logical consistency can seldom stir anyone as deeply as this kind of idealism.

Above all, we are given a new vindication for the life of religious inwardness against a world for which religion amounts to no more than its social functions. The dynamics of this thought reveal the influence of H.P. Blavatsky's dictum: 'There is no Religion above Truth,' but in a way which seeks to re-incorporate it into orthodoxy. It includes the vital ideas that truth itself has rights; that the authentic person is not necessarily obligated to society; that the work of truth is mystically effectual, both in the individual and in the outside world at the same time; that attachment to the Highest is the highest obligation.

With these principles, we have a solution to the modern spiritual crisis caused by the increasing adaptation of culture and religion to minds which are opposed to the spirit, making it part of a prevailing union of ignorance with power. Without the traditionalist option as outlined by Guénon, there could be no more resistance to the trend of stripping religion of its metaphysical elements and turning it into a psychological war against the intellect, which by a horrid irony, can present itself as coming from God. Inevitably this is hardest to bear for those who are capable of more than a faith made to fit the limitations of the modern mentality, and who have the most spiritual potentialities. Even though it is mingled with an utterly inadequate idea of the self, the point of view of this minority is now articulated, and in a way that profane culture cannot answer.

6

Platonism in Christianity

Universal Origins

I wish to approach the subject of Platonism in Christianity in a way which will distinguish it from other philosophical combinations, such as Christian Aristotelianism or Christian Existentialism. The very name 'Christian Platonism' is liable to suggest that it is simply one of a series of adaptations made with different philosophies for the purpose of adapting the religious message to different cultural conditions. While that was relevant to Christianity and Platonism in the early centuries AD, their relationship has remained meaningful long after Platonism ceased to be a major cultural force in society as a whole, and this is something which needs to be explained.

It is generally accepted that Christianity cannot in the long term be identified with any product of secular culture, however brilliant, and still be true to itself. How, then, are we to understand the idea that Platonism ought to be an exception to this rule, and have a privileged position in Christian thought, and in that of other religious traditions as well? Can it speak the language of the Spirit without being a part of revelation? To answer such questions, it will be necessary to look back over the origins of Plato's philosophy, so as to be able to see where he was, and where he was not, an innovator. This will, I hope, dispel the suspicion that what we have to do with here is just one more product of human ingenuity.

The history of archaic civilizations and cultures shows countless instances which illustrate the great antiquity of the idea that some realities are archetypes which confer meaning and power on communities and social activities which express something of them in their cultural forms. Not only is this common to nearly all ancient civilizations, it is also common to the even more numerous cultures which are normally classified as primitive. According to Mircea Eliade, a leading authority on comparative religion, for primitive man, 'an object or an act becomes real only insofar as it imitates or repeats an archetype.'[1]

Cities, and other man-made constructions were intentionally modelled on patterns seen among the stars. This is because, from a more sense-bound perspective, the spiritual archetype was often equated with something in the visible heavens. The ground-plans of temple-complexes provide examples which show that in very early times, things were done according to the idea that there were at least two distinct orders of reality, and that the lower of the two had to be in some sense a duplicate of the higher if it was to be effectual for its purpose. This is also true of ancient Egypt, where the regions or 'Nomes' are an example of planning on earth following patterns seen in the stars. Likewise, the building of Nineveh by Sennacherib was guided by a stellar pattern which was said to have been seen 'from distant ages.'

An equally emphatic example of ancient archetypalism can be seen in the British Museum, where there are illustrated Egyptian texts dating from around 1700 BC concerning the journey of a deceased person into the after-life. This person is shown discovering, among other things, the eternal River Nile, of which the earthly one is only a copy. If Greek wisdom was shown to be of Egyptian origin, therefore, it would not be very surprising.

In Jewish tradition, the idea that earthly things are copies of eternal ones appears in the Wisdom of Solomon, where the temple which Solomon is told to build is said to be 'a copy of the holy tent which thou didst prepare from the beginning' (Wis.9:8). Moses had already had the Ark of the Covenant and the Tabernacle made 'according to the pattern of what was shown him on the Mount.' Moreover, the eternal Ark of the Covenant is seen to appear in the

1. *The Myth of the Eternal Return*, tr. W.R. Trask (New York: Arkana, 1989), p34.

heavens, Apocalypse (Rev. 11:9), and in the same book, the New Jerusalem is seen descending to earth from God.

Plato himself speaks in a clearly similar manner in the *Republic* concerning his ideal city, where he says that, although it is not to be found on earth, it is 'perhaps laid up in heaven as a pattern for him who wills to see, and seeing, found a city in himself.'[2] Returning to Mircea Eliade, it appears that the same kind of thinking is to be found in ancient Iranian tradition, for which, he says, 'every terrestrial phenomenon, whether abstract or concrete, corresponds to a celestial, transcendent and invisible term.... Our earth corresponds to a celestial earth.' Thus there is a higher or metaphysical form of reality and a lower, or sensory form of it. The metaphysical reality is referred to as *Menok*, and the visible or phenomenal as *Getik*.[3] Thus, for example, the visible (*Getik*) heavens were taken to be the manifestation of the invisible (*Menok*) heavens. Subject to this conception, we could say that the ways in which the earth moves in space and on its axis are as though designed to produce the appearance of the visible heavens in a way which best symbolizes the eternal heavens. Creation would thus be accomplished twice over, that is, on two different levels.

Where the primitive peoples are concerned, Eliade observes that all life's important acts were 'revealed *ab origine* by gods or heroes. Men only repeat these exemplary and paradigmatic gestures *ad infinitum*.'[4] In innumerable cases where practical activities are ritualized, 'reality is acquired solely through repetition, or participation.' Failure to connect with an exemplary model is to fall into the meaningless. In religion, this thinking applies to all its aspects, not least in the way in which the events of salvation history are celebrated in the Church's liturgical year.

Where the ancient concept of archetypes affected the details of people's lives, or the forms of those details, it involved the paradoxical assumption that people had to become in some ways different

2. *Republic* 592B.

3. Mircea Eliade, ibid., pp6–7, 'Celestial Archetypes of Territories, Temples, and Cities'.

4. Ibid., p34, 'Archetypes of Profane Activities'.

from what they were in order to become more truly and fully what they were. As long as behavior is identified with its short-term practicalities alone, personal identity is felt to be scattered and all but lost to itself. Conversely, conformity to a type served to bring the outer self back into relation with its own essence. If personality is seen as a union of inner self and ego, an alteration to the ego in a way which is strongly expressive of the inner self will serve to integrate them, as like attracts like.

It should be noted that these archetypal realities adopted by archaic cultures were believed to have an independent power of their own, that is, their uses were not the same as human preferences for some selected historical events. In our materialistic culture, this kind of preference is only to be seen in the activities of historical re-enactment societies, which exclude themselves from the spiritual dimension by their openly human and social point of view. In this connection, I would add that, on an Aristotelian basis, there would be no escape from this position; the realities contained in salvation history would have no more transcendent being and reality of their own than would any purely historical events. Their archetypal reality would exist solely in the actions of priests and other Christians in celebrating them.

Pythagoras

This ancient archetypalist idea of reality was to be taken up with major developments by Plato, but the transition from this stage to the philosophy of Plato was still too large to be made in one move. What was missing was an understanding of the way in which the Forms or archetypes could operate in individual minds. So far, we have considered how they operated in society by generally qualifying the behavior of everyone in that society. Here, the role of the individual was mainly passive, since his activities did not necessarily require more than compliance with rules. The mediator who made possible the transition from this level of understanding was Pythagoras, who studied under the priests of the Semitic religions of the Near East, especially in Egypt.

While most people have heard of Pythagoras and his theorem,

the historical significance of the theorem is usually missed, or at least under-rated. Nevertheless, it is here that we find the epistemological revolution without which Plato's work could not have begun. Before the time of Pythagoras, practical geometrical problems were solved on a purely individual basis, and one of the commonest causes of such problems was the annual flooding of the Nile, which made it necessary to recalculate lengths of boundaries and areas of fields. In this context, the advent of theorems revealed that there were whole classes of problems capable of the same method of solution. This had the effect of liberating knowledge from the practical problems in which it had so long been immersed, and problems which had once seemed quite different from one another could now be seen to be subject to a single principle valid for all of them.

From this came the educational programme centered on arithmetic, geometry, music and astronomy, which was also to be adopted by Plato. The purifying effect of mathematics clearly came from the way in which it brought the mind into contact, not with things, so much as the essences of things, even though these essences were conceived as purely and simply mathematical, and not as any more universal reality, as with Plato, who saw mathematics as a preparation for knowledge of a more subtle kind, one which embraced both quantitative and qualitative principles equally. At last, the mind now knew itself to be able to transcend particulars and be more than a register of sense-objects.

The followers of Pythagoras found that this transcendence of particular cases had a similarly liberating effect on those who acquired this kind of knowledge, the mathematical form of which was to come to its full flowering with Euclid. This kind of liberation led to a deeper understanding of the difference between the natural world and the realm of ideas and values. The interaction between these modes of reality was shown to be operative in the mind of the individual, and thus not confined to the ritual and cultural forms employed by society. A new meaning and value for the individual was thus discovered in this role of mediator between two different orders of reality, and such is the function which is included in the idea of *Logos*. *Logos* in general signifies an absolute reality which is also inseparable from its productions or manifestations. This is a reality in which transcendence and immanence are specially combined, and are fused but not confused. This presupposes a real duality, while the terms of the duality are united in the operating Logos itself.

The *Logos* function of the soul and the microcosm doctrine each imply the other. Only a being who is so complex as to recapitulate all the different levels of being in the world could exert a mediating function between those levels. Conversely, the *Logos* function demands a being who is internally conversant with different orders of reality.

This development was accompanied by a number of related insights among the Pythagoreans, including the immortality of the soul and rewards and punishments in the hereafter, as well as in the idea of man as a microcosm. The writings of Hippocrates, who was a Pythagorean, bear witness to the presence of the idea of man as being a little world, and this idea, which makes the individual in some sense equivalent to the world, was later on to play its part in the Christian belief in the redemption of the world through Christ's Incarnation.

This metaphysical conception of the individual clearly deepens our understanding of the teaching that 'by one man sin came into the world,' and that 'by one man' the world was redeemed. We should note in passing that for Vedantic, or rather Shankaran, spirituality, this idea of God as being a mediator between Himself and creation must be meaningless, because it recognizes no reality between the Godhead and the realm of *Maya*; it thus can have no place for the Divine *Logos* or for the Trinity.

The theoretical vindication of what is thus a contradiction for some Vedantists was to emerge from another development of Pythagorean thought, one which was to show how the finite could have a positive meaning in relation to the infinite. The Pythagoreans drew up a list of pairs of opposites, which they believed to express the essential nature of the universe, and one such pair, which was to have particular importance in Greek thought later on, was that of the Limit and the Infinite, i.e., the *Peras* and the *Apeiron*, which is the first of ten pairs, of which all the others are taken to be manifestations. It was part of this intellectual revolution that the idea of the Limit was found to have a positive meaning, having as much or more than that of the Infinite. In the midst of all the mathematical thinking that went on, this showed that the merely quantitative view of reality was being transcended, and that there was a qualitative principle which was equal to anything in the order of quantity. In connection with the role of theorems in problem-solving, their reduction of a multitude of different problems to a single method of solution is a prime example of the victory of the Limit (or *Peras*) over the Infinite (or *Apeiron*), in which order and form can be seen to govern the apparently lawless. Being itself, for Platonism, was the result of the union of these two principles.[5]

The Limit and the Infinite are of fundamental importance for other things as well, both metaphysical and theological. In the latter connection, they are at the heart of the question as to why God should, or must, become man. Since the finite is not nothing, firstly because of its qualitative meaning, and secondly because, quantitatively, it is still infinitely more than nothing, the realization of the True Infinite requires a combination of what one could call the 'pure infinite' with the finite. Since the True Infinite is the ultimate reality, nothing can prevent its manifestation, and this was accomplished, therefore, by the Incarnation.

Another reason for the necessity of the Incarnation appears from the fact that if God were solely a pure spirit, man would in some sense be more than God, since he is a spirit who is also united with all the material levels of being. But this would be absurd, not least in view of the principle that man is made in the image of God. Consequently, what is a mediating function in man between the intellect and the natural order is, in Christ, a mediation between God and the whole of creation. The incarnation of the Divine *Logos* awakens the *Logos* principle in the individual person, saving it from being a mere potentiality.

In other words, the *Logos* in man resides paradigmatically in God, and, like all paradigms, will necessarily be made manifest in the cosmos. It should also be noted that the Greek culture in which

5. Proclus, *Elements of Theology*, prop. 89. E.R. Dodds, tr., Oxford, 1963.

such ideas arose was one in which God, or more generally the Divine, was conceived as being by nature open to all who wished to contemplate it. In this way, it was a culture which was as it were pre-adjusted to the Incarnation, therefore. This contrasts with Judaism and the other Semitic traditions, for which God was above all a hidden God, and for which spiritual wisdom was therefore secret. Here, then, is another reason why the Incarnation was mostly felt to be intolerable to the Jews, while being acceptable in the Gentile world.

This is far from exhausting the consequences of the metaphysics of the Limit and the Infinite, the *Peras* and the *Apeiron*, since they are also central in regard to the reasons why the Forms instantiate in matter, and why creation should be ordered in the manner of the Great Chain of Being. The reasons for the deep differences between Eastern and Western ideas of spiritual wisdom are to be found here as well. In what follows, I shall apply these ideas to the Principle of Plenitude, which is a name given to the manner in which Platonism conceives the formation of the Great Chain of Being.

The Great Chain of Being

From the point of view of Christian doctrine, and that of most other religions, an aspect of Plato's work which is spiritually just as important as the theory of Forms is the light it sheds on the Great Chain of Being. The theory of its formation was first expressed by Plato, and then much more fully by Plotinus and Proclus, but the principle involved never had a name, until the Nineteen Thirties, when A.O. Lovejoy called it the Principle of Plenitude. Platonism gives much theoretical insight into this subject, as I shall try to show.

The universality of the Great Chain of Being has been observed by a present-day authority on comparative religion, Huston Smith. Not only is it common to the Theistic religious traditions, it is also common to Oriental religions, including Buddhism, which does not believe in a personal God. Ken Wilber cites a number of other authorities who agree on this issue:

> According to this nearly universal view, reality is a rich tapestry of interwoven levels, *reaching from matter to body to mind to soul to spirit.* Each senior level 'envelops' or 'enfolds' its junior dimensions—a series of nests within nests of Being.[6]

At its simplest, this means that the body-soul-spirit constitution of the human being is matched by the existence of objective spiritual, psychical, and material worlds, arranged in a hierarchical order. These three cosmic levels have their sub-divisions, and all are expressive of different degrees of power and goodness. They range from the most universal and absolute to the most limited and ephemeral, traversing at the same time successively more gross forms of matter. The minimal group of types of beings corresponding to these levels would thus be bodies, souls, and spirits or intellects, where bodies are wholly subject to space and time, souls to time, but not to space, and intellects to neither.

The subdivisions of these orders of being are most familiar on the physical level, where the order of living species can be seen to range in a chain of complexity between mankind at one extreme, and life-forms on the edge of the inorganic, like viruses, at the other. The deep barriers and dualities involved in this are nevertheless balanced by the way in which our own nature comprises a synthesis of them all. Some things in man correspond to the inorganic, others to the vegetal creation, others to the animal state, and others again to the various orders of angels, besides the level which is specifically human. Every relation to some higher or lower element in the cosmic hierarchy involves a corresponding relation to its equivalent in oneself. Every attraction to God brings the individual into a closer relation to his own higher possibilities at the same time, therefore, without that dividing his spiritual possibilities from his natural ones.

This was the idea which had been emerging in Pythagorean thought, and which was further developed by Plato and Plotinus. Its relevance to the understanding of Christ's role as the one being

6. Ken Wilber, *The Marriage of Sense and Soul* (Boston: Shambhala Publications, 2001), pp 6–7.

in whom the whole natural order was to be regenerated, has already been indicated. The more it is understood how one being can in some sense be equivalent to the All, the more meaning is to be seen in the redemption of the world in Christ, and so also in human lives, insofar as they find grace.

According to the Platonists, the Great Chain of Being comes into being through the instantiation of Forms, but we cannot simply take it for granted without explanation that Forms must necessarily instantiate themselves, in this way or any other. For this purpose we need to consider the way in which Plato arrived at the Form of the Good. While each of the other Forms was the ideal pattern and generative principle for all the individual instances of it that appeared in the outside world, the same way of thinking about the Forms themselves led to the idea of a super-Form which was a cause of all the other Forms, as they are of their instantiations, and which gave order and unity to them and to all that followed from them.

This unifying function is to be seen, not only in the unity of the natural order, but even in the way in which our minds come to know the truth. It is through the mediation of the Form of the Good that the mind has access to the ideas, and it is here that we find the Platonic roots of the idea of the Divine illumination of the mind.

The Form of the Good has a perfection which logically implies self-sufficiency, so that the only way of going beyond it or adding to it must lie not in itself but in other and lesser beings which are made as much like it as possible. If the Good were not productive, it would be lacking in a perfection, but since it is by definition perfect, it must be productive. But can these lesser realities really add anything to the Supreme, or have any reality of their own? There are religious traditions which would answer this in the negative, even though they admit the Great Chain of Being in some sense or other. They would say that the reality of the One must exclude that of the many.

But Plato did not stop at so simple an answer as this. He was following the tradition for which the Limit is in its own way as real as the Infinite, according to the principles already discussed in connection with the way in which Greek (and probably Egyptian) thought perceived the qualitative reality of the finite.

This time, however, the union of these two realities, because of the equal necessity of the finite, constitutes a generative principle by which the Good brings about all lower orders of being without any direct substantive transfer from itself. Together with the Good, these relative beings manifest the True Infinite, which is reflected in the idea of God according to negative theology, where this includes both every affirmation and the negation of every affirmation. In this context, the Incarnation affirms the meaning and power of the finite as the qualitative counterpart of the 'pure' infinite.

The consequences of this are momentous for religion, since the supremely other-worldly reality now becomes the source of innumerable other realities, that is, of entities which are not simply the play of illusion, because all degrees of real being are distributed in them. The absolute barrier between God and creation is overcome in a way that is far more sophisticated than the way in which this is done by pantheism, which would simply conflate them. Such is the idea which Plato introduces in the *Timaeus*. Here, he uses the idea of what he calls the 'Living Creature' to denote the integral sum of all the Forms which are instantiated in the material world:

> What was the living creature in whose likeness he constructed the world? We cannot allow that it was any that ranks only as a species; for no copy of that which is incomplete can ever be good. Let us rather say that the world resembles most closely that Living Creature of which all other living creatures severally and in their families are parts. For that embraces and contains within itself all the intelligible living creatures, just as this world contains ourselves and all other creatures that have been fashioned as visible things.[7]

Creation is thus seen as the realization on the material level of all the possibilities already realized in the Forms. If we think of it in terms of time, we could say that what came 'first' was what was by nature closest to the Good, and subsequently, things which were successively less like it, thus giving rise to the Great Chain of Being. Not only does the material world duplicate the intelligible world,

7. *Timaeus* 30C–31A, John Warrington, tr. (London: J.M. Dent & Sons, 1965).

but this kind of duplication is not confined to one instance, since the Principle of Plenitude implies its repetition at other ontological levels. In this connection, we should consider the four levels of being according to the Kabbalah: Atziluth, Briah, Yetzirah, and Assiah, each of which comprises the same realities according to its own property. In a similar way, Proclus subdivides human existence into four material levels, where the matter of the first is of fire, then of air, then of water, and lastly of earth, that being our own level in this conception of the universal order. Each of these successively lower levels is necessary to create continuity, as the Great Chain descends from the purely intellectual and immaterial man, down to the lowest and most mutable enmattered man.[8]

Sources for the Idea of Plenitude

One implication of the Principle of Plenitude is that all possibilities, where they are practically possible in combination with other possibilities, must eventually be realized in the world. Inferior possibilities would have just as much right to realization as superior ones. According to Plotinus, objecting to this

> is like complaining because one kind of animal lacks horns. We ought to understand both that the Reason-Principle must extend to every possible existent and, at the same time, that every greater must include lesser things. . . .[9]

Inequality is in effect the condition under which things can exist at all, as though 'to be' had to mean the same as 'to be different', which appears more explicitly from what follows in the *Enneads*:

> And since the higher exists, there must be the lower as well. The Universe is a thing of variety, and how could there be an inferior without a superior or a superior without an inferior? We cannot

8. Proclus' Commentary on Plato's *Parmenides*, Bk III, 812, G.R. Morrow and J.M. Dillon, trs. (Princeton: Princeton University Press, 1987).

9. *Enneads*, III, 2, 14, MacKenna tr., 1962.

complain about the lower in the higher; rather we must be grateful to the higher for giving something of itself to the lower.[10]

Similarly, he says:

the plurality of beings, offspring of the unity, could not exist without their own nexts taking the outward path; . . . in the same way the outgoing process could not end with souls, their issue stifled: every Kind must produce its next; it must unfold from some concentrated principle as from a seed, and so advance to its term in the varied forms of sense. The prior in its being will remain unalterable in its native seat; but there is the lower phase, begotten to it by an ineffable faculty of being, native to soul as it exists in the supreme[11].

In this last passage, Plotinus dissociates the Principle of Plenitude from emanation, as taken in the pantheistic sense, where the dependent beings require an actual transfer of substance from the higher one. On the contrary, this conception requires each higher power to generate the next lower outside itself in a way that has no effect on its own power. This aspect of the process has been called the principle of 'Undiminished Giving', by Paul Henry in his Introduction to the *Enneads*,[12] and it is an essential property of Plenitude which distinguishes it from all materialistic and pantheistic conceptions. This also accounts for what could be called a 'one-sided relation' between Forms and their instantiations, where the Form is in no way affected in itself by its instantiations, whether they be few or many, long-lasting or transient. Plotinus expresses this idea as follows:

A widespread activity is dangerous to those who must go out from themselves to act. But such is the blessedness of this Being that in its very non-action it magnificently operates, and in its self-dwelling it produces mightily.[13]

This idea is applied by St Thomas Aquinas in his sermon on the

10. *Enneads*, III, 3, 7
11. *Enneads*, IV, 8, 6.
12. Ibid., p LX.
13. *Enneads*, III, 2, 1,

Body of the Lord which, he says is eaten, but like the burning bush, not consumed, and neither in itself is divided or broken.[14] The idea of Plenitude is also made use of by Aquinas, as will appear presently.

There is, then, no question of any mingling of cause with effect, or any wearing out of the cause, such as happens in physical causality. What the spiritual and natural orders of causality do have in common, though, is a systematic reduction in the scope of their activity. Among the Forms, none can produce another equal to, or greater than itself, and among physical causes, something of the power of the cause is always lost as it produces its effects. This goes back to the fact that God cannot produce a second God, since there can only be one Absolute.

The theory which this involves has been discussed in more detail by Proclus, in his series of theorems on causality:

> Whatever is complete proceeds to generate those things which it is capable of producing, imitating in its turn the one originative principle of the universe.[15]

Whatever exists has, *ipso facto* some causal power, and the only exception to this is the material principle, which is the last and least real of all things. Like Plotinus, he says: 'Every productive cause produces the next and all subsequent principles while itself remaining steadfast.' (Prop. 26). But now Proclus proceeds to a development of this idea which is crucial for the Great Chain of Being: 'Every producing cause brings into existence things like to itself before the unlike.'[16]

This implies that there can be no voids in either the physical or the spiritual universe, so that it may appear that there should be only the tiniest differences between the different kinds of being which exist together. However, there is nothing in this conception to determine which members of the Chain of Being will be contiguous with, or even contemporaneous, with which. The universe, like

14. 'Sermon on the Body of the Lord', *Thomas Aquinas, Selected Writings*, M.C. D'Arcy, S.J., ed.,(London: J.M. Dent, 1964).

15. *Elements of Theology*, Prop. 25.

16. Ibid., Prop. 28.

an organism, is composed of relative unities or 'holons', themselves ordered in hierarchies, and such parts of the world as these need no more than a representative selection from the total range of being in order to reflect the Whole. This procession of being and reality is therefore distributed over many orders of being, some close to the divine, such that they share to a large degree in God's self-existence, and some so remote that they are contingencies purely and simply, like dust in the wind, although man is capable of rising to higher places in this order. What issues from God in this way is subject to a progressive attenuation until it ends with the material principle itself, a property which is illustrated by the Scholastics with a comparison with the heat from a fire. When one is closest to the fire, the heat does not differ from the heat in the fire in itself, while the heat is continuously reduced in proportion to the distance away from the fire. Another way of representing it would be by comparison with an artefact like a garment or tool which does fully what it is intended to do when new, but gradually less so as it wears out.

From quite early times, this idea of a hierarchy of being was an accepted means of explaining the world for Christian thinkers as much as for non-Christian. St Augustine gives an unqualified affirmation of it which includes a new way of illustrating it. He uses it here as a way of answering the problem of evil:

> I will say . . . that the orderly arrangement of creatures extends all the way from the highest good to the lowest according to just gradations in such a way that only envy could prompt a man to say that a creature should not exist, or that it should be different. For if he wants it to be the same as something higher, then such a creature is already existing and possesses such excellence that nothing more should be added, since it is perfect in its kind. If he maintains that the lower creature should also have this excellence, he either wants to add to the higher, which is already perfect . . . or he want to destroy the lower creature. . . .[17]

He goes on to explain that to make the lower being into a copy of

17. *The Free Choice of the Will*, bk. 3, chap. 9, R.P. Russel, O.S.A., tr. (Washington, DC: Catholic University of America Press, 1968).

the higher is just as destructive an act as to make the higher into a copy of the lower. Harmony comes from the interaction between truly different entities, and equality prevents that. This is supported by a comparison with the Sun and the Moon:

> Now if he does not deny that the Moon should exist, but says that it should be like the Sun, he fails to realize that he is merely saying that there should be two Suns and no Moon. Here he is doubly mistaken: he wants to add to the perfection of the universe by desiring another Sun and to detract from its perfection by taking away the Moon.[18]

In other words, one would be adding something which did not really add anything, except in a merely numerical manner, and at the same time taking away something else which really did do so, because it realized a new possibility. Perfection cannot be produced by repetition or purely quantitative multiplication. An infinitely powerful Creator could have no motive for repetition, and from this follows the uniqueness of every personality.

This is an insight which pantheistic spiritualities cannot include. For them, the lesser degree of perfection is no perfection at all, because their ideas do not offer any challenge to the quantitative common sense idea that the finite can only be a negligible bit of the infinite, and not an equal principle of being in its own right. This is why the Great Chain of Being is as necessary for Christian doctrine as for Platonism. The meaning it allows to personality is also connected with the way in which the person is a synthesis of the All; the absolute Unity is mirrored and recapitulated in endless different ways in all relative created beings.

St Thomas Aquinas also bears witness to the central importance of the Chain of Being, even though with certain reservations, owing, among other things, to the fact that its 'outgoing' perspective needs to be balanced for devotional purposes by the opposite one of conversion or reascent to the Divine. Aquinas approaches it from the position that what God wills absolutely is His own nature, which is alone of all things worthy of that. However, it follows from this that

18. Ibid.

other things must be loved and willed as well to a lesser degree, where these are all the beings which reflect the Divine nature to some degree or other:

> the things that we love for their own sake we want to be most perfect, and always to become better and be multiplied as much as possible. But God wills and loves His own essence for its own sake. Now the divine essence cannot be increased or multiplied in itself, as it can be multiplied solely according to its likeness, which is participated by many. God therefore wills the multitude of things in willing and loving His own essence and perfection.[19]

In the same place, he goes on to argue that, in willing Himself, God must necessarily will everything that archetypally exists in Him, which would comprise an innumerable multitude of creatures. He also shows that beings produce more numerous and more remote effects in proportion to the greatness of their causal power, which implies that God must create all orders of being without omitting any, with a necessity which is related to the necessity by which God is good, i.e., a necessity which appears in the fact that God could not be more free by being bad as well as good.

This necessity is denied elsewhere by Aquinas on the grounds that creation in fact does not add anything to God; God must by definition be independent of all relative beings. This can sound rather strange, however, in view of the fact that we have just seen it argued that God's perfection *does* require the existence of the creation. Lovejoy simply observes that Aquinas both affirms and denies the Principle of Plenitude, without trying to explain why. There is apparently no attempt to resolve the question in these texts of Aquinas, but in view of what has been considered before, it can be seen that this is a case where contradictory attributes can be affirmed of God, both of which would be equally true. God cannot be understood through any one rational construction, even though aspects of God can be.

To help clarify this evident contradiction, we should consider

19. *SCG*, 1, 75, [3], *On the Truth of the Catholic Faith*, Anton C. Pegis, tr., (Doubleday & Co., 1955).

infinity, the finite, and zero together. It can be seen that, from one point of view, the finite must be nothing in relation to the infinite, while from another point of view it cannot really be nothing, because it is infinitely more than zero. Both of these perspectives are true, whence the ambivalent nature of creation. The problem here is aggravated by the idea of a hard opposition between a purely infinite God and a purely finite creation. This division is final for exoteric religion as such, but the esoteric resolves it by its exploration of the degrees of infinity possessed by created spiritual beings. Consequently, the nullity of creation in relation to God applies in full strictness only to the inanimate part of creation.

Elsewhere, Aquinas illustrates the Principle of Plenitude with the idea that God would create one angel and a stone, rather than two angels. According to the Principle, the correct answer must be one angel and a stone, and this highlights the fact that, according to the Principle, as Lovejoy puts it, 'the desirability of a thing's existence bears no relation to its excellence.' Plenitude, or the generation of the Great Chain of Being, is thus in itself not a moral or, more generally, axiological process. Mere possibility is enough to warrant actuality, granted only that the possibility is compatible with a sufficient number of other possibilities in the place assigned to it.

Conclusions

It will not have escaped notice that the Great Chain of Being is not a very fashionable idea today, and in fact its influence in our culture has been in retreat for two hundred years now. It has been generally rejected along with metaphysics itself, and at the same time the last two hundred years have seen an equally steady advance of secularism. This is by no means a coincidence. There are wider issues involved here, because much of the opposition to this idea is essentially political, and the reason for that is that one of its most direct consequences is that the differences and inequalities among people are created by God, just as much as they themselves are.

Instead of a cosmology which implies originality and real individuality, there is now a secular ideal which aims at making people as much as possible equal, as though everyone had to wish they were persons of a certain type. With the passage of time, therefore, the traditional ideal of becoming more like God has been displaced by an anti-ideal of becoming more like other people. This kind of change could only happen in a culture where first principles were taken to be merely a matter of human preference or convenience.

What exactly is at stake here? If modern thought was right, and Plenitude and the Great Chain of Being were only a human passion and not founded in the nature of things, the first consequence would be that the world could not be conceived as a theophany, having no intrinsic and systematic relation to God. This would point to the opposite alternative, the world of the Manichaeans, a kind of hell contrived by a demonic deity for the purpose of excluding us from God. In this case, metaphysical knowledge would be impossible, since there would be no divine order for it to relate to. This was why Plotinus attacked the Manichaean system at such length in his text *Against the Gnostics*.

In this case there would be no point in respect for nature, and no point in preferring the natural to the unnatural. The world could only rationally be treated as an accumulation of stuff which we could put to any purposes without any question of profanity. Do we not in fact see an implicit Manichaean tendency in much that is going on in modern culture? Among Idealists and activists there are those whose message bears an assumption that this world is a kind of disaster area from which we need to protect ourselves by ever more stringent and socially intrusive measures. Paradoxically, this attitude appears more markedly in proportion as life becomes more safe and physically comfortable.

An over-emphasis on the evil aspect of the world, and an excessive fear of it, involves a rejection of the idea that we are creatures under Providence. One implication of this idea is that we are the highest kind of being only in relation to the natural order, but the lowest in the hierarchy of spirits, and so even more obviously subordinate to God, since being subject to God is to be subject to God's order.

But modern man, having disowned the metaphysical interpretation of the world, and its different levels of being, rejects the idea that he is part of an order which was not devised by other human beings. Instead, he falls for the belief that he can be his own creator, and make all values and options the products and tools of his own will. The possibilities opened up by applied science are notoriously flattering to this attitude. But however alluring this is felt to be, it involves the absurdity of equating the relative with the absolute, that is, equating the human desires of a brief historical period with eternal verities. Besides, value, like truth itself, could not be value if we had the power to create or invent it. There is a choice here between chaos and cosmos, which is inevitably for chaos when this issue is not understood.

Some things taken for evils are in fact no more than the result of there being differences, together with the fact that in our present state we are not effectively joined to the archetypal principle by which God makes the world. The suppression of differences between individuals is also a suppression of their possibility of self-realization, since the latter can only grow from a genuine identity, the one with which they were created.

Granted the reality of the Chain of Being, there need be no problem with the validity of religious experience. Everything from personal experiences to theoretical proofs of God, which convince those who believe, are automatically well-founded in a world which is essentially a theophany, forming as a physical whole one link in a range of realities delegated downwards from God. Because of this systematic relation of the world to the Creator, faith and reason have ample grounds for being mutually supportive.

The immortality of the soul and the divinity of reason are inseparable from this Platonic cosmology, because the immortality of the soul is the measure of relative self-existence that belongs to man's place in the universal order, while reason is the light by which the cosmic law is made known to itself. These things have been implicit in nearly all formulations of Christian doctrine, at least up till about fifty years ago, when the traditional norm began to come under attack.

It should now be easier to see what close interrelations there are between the Incarnation, the Limit-and-the-Infinite, and the microcosm doctrine. Such are the principles of a spiritual world-view which integrates the spiritual with the natural. That is a cornerstone of religion which dominates the common ground between revealed religion and pure metaphysics.

Notes and Further Sources

Table of Opposites

Limit	Infinite
Odd	Even
Unity	Plurality
Right	Left
Male	Female
Rest	Motion
Straight	Crooked
Light	Darkness
Good	Evil
Square	Oblong

All these opposites after the first pair are manifestations of the Primal Pair, the Limit and the Infinite. (See *Philebus* 16c.) The Limit and the Infinite are what come first after the One, which is beyond all distinct concepts.[20]

Aquinas, regarding archetypal realities in God: 'Furthermore, in willing Himself, God wills all that is in Him. But all things in a certain manner pre-exist in Him through their proper models. . . .[21]

Aquinas denies the independent subsistence of the Forms, because he is an Aristotelian, but the subsistent Forms are a consequence of the Great Chain of Being (GCB), which Aquinas accepts.

The GCB has been supposed incompatible with the absolute freedom attributed to God. The problem in the belief in absolute freedom is whether it can be any more real than absolute determination, which does away with the thing determined? Absolute freedom could not be a freedom from anything, since it would exclude any context in which it could be exercised.

20. See Proclus, *In Eucl.* 1, 5). Also ref F.M. Cornford, *Plato and Parmenides*, pp6–7.

21. *SCG*, 1, chap. 75, [5].

Nicolaus Cusanus on the GCB:

> All things, however different, are linked together. There is in the genera of things such a connection between the higher and the lower that they meet in a common point; such an order obtains among species that the highest species of one genus coincides with the lowest of the next higher genus, in order that the universe may be one, perfect, continuous.[22]

If Absolute Perfection implies the production of lesser beings beyond itself, the omission of any possible form of being would be as much opposed to that Perfection as the failure to create anything at all. Only God is above the Limit and the Infinite, and God's absolute indetermination means that He must also possess a determinate nature to the fullest extent as well, or else the formal indetermination would be substantively a determination.

Proclus, concerning the Limit and the Infinite:

> To find the principles of mathematical being as a whole, we must ascend to those all-pervading principles that generate everything from themselves: namely the Limit and the Infinite. For these, the two highest principles after the indescribable and utterly incomprehensible causation of the One, give rise to everything else, including mathematical beings. . . . The objects of Nous, by virtue of their inherent simplicity, are the first partakers of the Limit and the Infinite. Their Unity, their identity, and their stable and abiding existence they derive from the Limit; but for their variety, their generative fertility, and their divine otherness and progression they draw upon the Infinite.[23]

Plato, on the Limit and the Infinite:

> A gift of heaven, which, as I conceive, the gods tossed among men by the hands of a new Prometheus, and therewith a blaze of light; and the ancients, who were our betters and nearer the gods than we are, handed down the tradition that whatever things are

22. *De Docta Ignorantia* III, 1.
23. *A Commentary on the First Book of Euclid's Elements*, Prologue, bk I, chap. II.

said to be composed of one and many, have the finite and the infinite implanted in them. . . .'[24]

One implication of this principle is that we must qualify St Augustine's contention that Platonism and the Western intellectual tradition had nothing corresponding to the Incarnation; the finite has its own ultimate reality.

24. *Philebus* 16c.

7

The Soul and Salvation

Whether Personal or Impersonal

Implicit in the idea of the salvation of the soul is the immortality of the soul, which is a necessary but not sufficient condition for its salvation. Consequently, the nature of both of these things will be considered in parallel, since they are closely involved with one another, and I shall show how the basic principles involved in them can lead to a Christian answer, or one which is open to Christian interpretation. The supernatural property of the soul can be understood in widely different ways, varying from that of an impersonal principle of consciousness ('divine spark', *Atman, Nous*) to that of a complete person. But in either case, it is understood to mean that the soul, or principle of the body's life and form, is a non-material substance, which is able to exist apart from its body. Though we may never have experienced a disembodied state, there are ways of showing that the soul has an independent nature which continues despite disembodiment.

Those who deny the idea that the person could be composed of such deeply different elements argue that what we call the embodied state of the soul is the only one ever known, and that soul and body are only aspects of the person, which cannot meaningfully be separated. This is to think as though the person was a composite like a green pigment, which could not remain when its blue or yellow component was removed. In this case, the union of body and soul would be like that between two material substances. This is one reason why empirical thinking finds an incoherence in the idea that our conscious self, the soul, could remain when its embodiment ceases at death even though death shows that the body is separable. Such thinking is relevant only for combinations between substances of the same kind, whereas body and soul differ by nature more deeply than do any two material substances. Consequently, this objection cannot be met until it is shown that man's conscious nature has properties which belong in a different category from the body and sense-experience, or from anything they could cause.

From an impersonal point of view, it is relatively easy to demonstrate the reality of an immortal principle in the self, as in Oriental traditions, where this would be one which could inhere equally in all conscious beings. A soul of this kind could reincarnate through innumerable successive bodies without this having any personal significance for any of those whose incarnated consciousness participated in it. Such a universal soul or self is of theoretical if not personal interest because of the part it plays in consciousness. Its basic properties were known also to Kant, who refers to it as the 'Synthetical Unity of Apperception',[1] where he examines it as the underlying level of consciousness by which the variety of objects in consciousness is grasped as a unity. The immortality of such a transcendental entity is no more a personal issue than the indestructibility of the ultimate particles which compose the body, and so it could not be a subject for salvation.

An essentially similar view of the self was also that of the Averroists, who drew a reductive conclusion from Aristotle's idea that there was but one intellect in all beings. The Synthetical Unity and the atoms of the body are the two simple extremes between which personality exists, and they are equally off-scale in relation to the possibilities of personality, which belongs to the most complex level of being. This is a realm which seems to consist wholly in processes in which things are built up by aggregation and destroyed by dispersion, and this shows why the immortality of a soul with personal attributes, recognizable as oneself, presents a harder problem than anything inherent in the *Nous* or Self.

1. *Critique of Pure Reason,* Transcendental Logic, First Division, chap. 2, §12, §13, J.M.D. Meiklejohn, tr. (London: J.M. Dent & Sons, 1956).

The Soul and Salvation

A Non-Personal Immortality

In *The Surangama Sutra*,[2] there is a discussion of consciousness which shows that it is not a thing with any spatial location, and so cannot be on the same level as any of its sensory contents. It is seen to transcend these contents in a manner which is consistent with the idea of the soul as a world-representing power. This is followed by another dialogue between the Buddha and King Prasenajit which focuses on changes which take place in the body as it ages. The king admits that his body is relentlessly changing for the worse all the time, instancing the changes in his health and appearance over the years. The Buddha then asks him if he thinks there is anything in him which would escape destruction when death came, and suggests an answer by asking when he first remembered being taken to bathe in the Ganges. He says that it was when he was aged three, and referred to some other occasions between then and the present time when he had bathed there; the Buddha asks him how the Ganges appeared to him on each of these occasions, and the king tells him that it looked the same each time, upon which the Buddha tells him that his 'perception of sight' has continued unchanged despite the increasing frailty of his body.

The duality indicated by this is unmistakable: unlike the body, the power of visual consciousness has neither youth nor age, so that it must 'survive to reappear in another body,' as the text puts it. This appears to be as far as Buddhism recognizes the immortality of the soul, and there is little or no personal significance in it. The simplicity and clarity with which one can demonstrate the transcendent reality of the 'perception of sight' or the *Atman*, as Hindus call it, can easily make one suppose that there is something equally evident in the conclusion that it is the final truth about our spiritual nature, a universal which can remain when all else has passed. There are, however, serious problems with the notion that one can identify exclusively with this principle in a state unrelated to any other. The belief in such a separation between the universal and the individual

2. See Wei-Tao and Dwight Goddard translation, chap. 4, from *The Wisdom of India*, 1965, Lin Yutang, ed.

self can be explained as a result of ignoring the way in which abstract thought can, in its own realm, separate things which are not separable in the objective world, and treat them in the same way as things which are so separable. An example of this is the distinction between Primary and Secondary qualities, like extension and color. For scientific purposes we can think of things which are extended while being without color, but in objective fact, there can no more be extension without color than color without extension. This is a typical pitfall of abstract thought where its limitations are not recognized.[3]

The Hindu idea of the immortal soul or self separates it in the same way as in the above, as is illustrated by Stephen Clark with a quotation from Shankara:

> Since the Self is the witness of the body, its acts, its states, therefore the Self must be of other nature than the body. . . . Of this compound of skin, flesh, fat, bone and water, the man of deluded mind thinks 'This is I'; but he who is possessed of judgement knows that his true Self is of other character, in nature transcendental.[4]

Here again, the person is understood in terms of a simple dichotomy between a more or less expendable material entity and a thing of real and absolute value, and again we are offered no basis for believing there to be any relation between them. To represent the person as composed of such remote and disparate extremes is to ignore the truth that the person comprises all levels of being, such that the highest spiritual principle and the purely material one are related by a continuum of states which reflects the Great Chain of Being in the individual. The soul is the substance in which this hierarchy of being resides, uniting the *Nous* at one extreme with the

3. A practical objection to this is that the separability of the essential principle of consciousness is not a matter of theory, but of mystical experience. But even though the core of consciousness be subjectively separated from its content in mystical states, this separation is neither substantive nor final, since it can be seen to form part of the biography of an individual who lives through it. True separation in this connection could only mean an all-too literal extinction.

4. *A Parliament of Souls*, Oxford, 1990, chap. 8, pp158–159.

body at the other. From this integration of levels of being comes the possibility of a spiritualization of the whole, in harmony with the Highest. Without this conception, one would have to say which part of the being achieves its identity with the Self or *Nous,* which if inferior to it would deny the Self's transcendence, and if equivalent to it would be redundant; in short, the question is unanswerable.

This shows that the separation of the *Nous* solves no problems, to say the least. The belief that the transcendental core of consciousness can be separated from the contents of consciousness and from the soul itself in objective fact, and not just conceptually, is as unwarrantable in its own way as the average common sense belief that the desirable contents of consciousness subsist independently of any higher unifying principle. Without its phenomenal content, the central principle would no longer have the same nature and *raison d'être,* as would also be the case if a Form could be made unable to cause any instantiations of itself.

Unlike the Oriental traditions, a Christian gnosis requires both 'poles' of consciousness, because belief in the Incarnation does not allow that the manifest personality is only a ladder to be kicked away when some unspecified entity has identified with the *Nous* or *Atman.* It therefore also implies that this central principle of consciousness and the phenomenal or individual self are not a choice, except by way of abstraction. Besides, there is no theoretical necessity for man to identify wholly with the *Nous,* just because the latter is transcendental in relation to the phenomenal self. The finite is an ultimate principle symmetrical with the pure infinite, because the true Infinite requires both the pure infinite and the finite, as in the relation of the Limit and Infinite at the head of the Pythagorean table of opposites.

It is specifically in the mortal part of the personality that the need for sanctification and salvation becomes observable, even though it actually takes place in the invisible soul; but the non-Christian idea of a salvation involving only a spiritual principle which has no need of it is really a denial of the idea of salvation in any meaningful form. While this belief is motivated by a high and austere ideal which appeals to a deep asceticism of the mind, if not of the body, it cannot subsist with the belief that the human state as a whole has been united with God in Christ, in Whom it is to be resurrected. The divergence involved here shows that one can be a complete idealist without what Christian orthodoxy would call faith or grace, even though an essential but limited truth may be held without them. The problem with this position is that it will not advance beyond the basic dichotomy of the body and the intellectual principle. While this by itself obviously does not suffice for any personal immortality, or for an account of the whole person, it is nevertheless a necessary stage in the process of proving that the individual soul has a transcendental reality of its own, which is not simply the same as that of the intellect.

Plotinus and the Soul's Transcendence

The impassive and unchanging component of consciousness was allowed its full importance by Plotinus, who discusses it in connection with experiences of pain and suffering.[5] Plotinus discriminates between a sensory (*aisthetikon*) phase of the soul and the soul's rational (*logikon*) knowledge of its condition; this sensitive power mediates between the spiritual principle and the body. What we call pain (or pleasure) is a blend of these two modes of consciousness, which are nevertheless separable for thought. While the pain is in just one part of the body, it is known but not suffered by the whole soul, which is wholly present to every such part. Here he makes the point that the mind must always remain unaffected by all the physical conditions it registers, if it is truly to know them.

The consciousness of pain belongs, it is said, to the sensitive phase of the soul, which communicates it to the imaging principle, which is the common center of all kinds of sense experience. If the rationally-conscious soul were affected by pain, the pain would be felt throughout the body, inasmuch as the soul is present to every part of the body. We should not be able to locate the pain in any place, and the soul

5. *Enneads* IV, 4, 19. MacKenna translation, Faber & Faber, 1962.

> [w]ould suffer as one entire being, so that it could not know, or make known, the spot affected; it could say only that at the place of its presence there existed pain - and the place of its presence is the entire human being.[6]

Moreover, if the cognitive (*noetikon*) function of the soul could be so affected, its knowledge would cease to be trustworthy, leading to the paradox that the pain could mean that we were not really in pain at all. The more violent the shocks sustained, the more clearly exempt the mind must be from them, if it is to have a veridical experience.

In the case of pains which originate mentally, from reflection upon experience, they really do pervade our whole being. Must this not conflict with the idea that the soul transcends pain and pleasure? In fact it only conflicts with the supposition that the whole soul, in all its functions, transcends pain, because its cognitive faculties still have to operate in the same exempt manner in the case of mental distress. Otherwise, here again, we should not be able to know that the mental distress was real.

The issue of mental suffering, however, reflects the fact that the soul cannot be a simple or homogenous entity because, in addition to its relation to intellect, it comprises a level of conscious activity which is adapted to the conditions of the body, and which therefore has its own equivalents of physical pains or pleasures. Since this sensitive 'part' ('parts' here meaning diversities of function) of the soul forms a continuum with the intellectual and rational 'parts', there is no reason why it should participate any less than the latter in the possibility of immortality, even though not automatically; the soul's complexity does not destroy its unity, and all its levels of awareness are equally parts of its world-representation. This is where the argument diverges from Oriental thought and some kinds of Aristotelian thought, since they see only the intellectual core of the soul as immortal.

In thinking this way, they ignore the fact that the intellectual 'part' of the soul, that is, its power of communing directly with

6. Ibid.

intellect,[7] is separable from the other 'parts' only by its functions, and not substantively, this being the same issue referred to above in connection with the 'perception of sight' or *Atman* as a supposedly separable reality. When the distinctions possible for thought are confused with concrete distinctions in such cases, it is as though a distinction between fire and its heat was treated as though it were like that between oil and water.

The spirituality of the soul is manifest even in sense perception, because each one of the five senses delivers a sensory diversity to a single center which perceives the senses themselves and coordinates them so that one knows that it is the same thing which is seen, heard, felt, and so on. This center is truly a unity because, if it had parts, all its sensory knowledge would be parcelled out into fragments of awareness with no awareness of one another. Instead, the innumerable tiny elements of each sensation are all gathered into a unity in which their differences can be known. Such a 'partless part' as this could not by any means be a material thing.

The communication of sensations through the body is likewise conducted by a unity which is present as a whole throughout it, and not as being partially present in each part of the body. Suppose this were not true, and that pain, say, was communicated from the part affected to the next part adjacent to it, and from that to the one next to it, and so on till the center of consciousness was reached: in this case, the latter would only be aware of the pain-impression of the part nearest it, and not where the pain really was. Yet this is how it would have to be if sensory awareness was conveyed on a material basis.

These ideas can be extended to thought, where it is concerned with things which are in themselves unextended, like most of the concepts used in philosophical reasoning. As Plotinus expresses it, thinking cannot depend on any function of the body if it is different from sensation at all. In this realm there are countless things for which the idea of size is meaningless, so that it is doubly

7. The possibility of intellectual error results from the fact that this function of the soul is not actually the same as intellect itself, even though, unlike the will, it cannot resist truth indefinitely, as Schuon points out.

inconceivable that they could be processed by an instrument of consciousness which had any size of its own:

> how then will something which is a size think what is not a size and think what is partless with something which has parts?[8]

Thoughts thus arise specifically through an act of separation from the body and from any material context, and where they involve truths, they can be known to be eternal and universal, properties which again are not possible for any material substance. This partless and sizeless power is nevertheless able to grasp the extended and divided contents of the senses and impose a relative unity on them by making them into a complex whole. For this reason the soul is in a sense both divisible and indivisible, from whence arises its function as mediating principle or *logos* between body and intellect. In this role it is an individual reflection of the mediating role of the Universal *Logos* between the transcendent unity of God and the creation as a whole.

On the one hand, the soul undergoes change inasmuch as it registers changes in the things it knows, and on the other hand it is beyond change, inasmuch as its activity is not subject to any entropy, weakening or diminution with the passage of time. This does not apply to the whole person, of course; it does not mean that our natural faculties must stay equally strong throughout life, because the natural faculties depend on interactions between the soul and various organs of the body, which cannot be free from change. But the fact that the practical powers of the person are limited by the age and health of the body, does not imply any such mutability in the interior source of their function.

An example of this can be seen in the way in which the eye may become blind, owing to some treatable cause. If the eye is healed, and sight is restored, it is made clear that the visual faculty had remained unchanged, but was now able to act through the eye again. The same in principle, if not in actual fact, applies to the brain. Deterioration in its physical condition blocks the activity of the conscious being in the outside world, even though this activity

8. *Enneads* IV, 7, 8.

is unchanged in itself. A restoration of the earlier state of the brain would therefore result in the re-manifestation of the same mind and personality as before, which had only been imprisoned, so to speak, by organic deficiencies. Such facts as these follow naturally from what was argued concerning the visual power in the *Surangama Sutra*, and from the argument of Plotinus that we only know pain because our knowledge does not itself suffer, which extends its scope for the purpose of self-awareness; failure in the powers of the soul itself can no more be produced by physical causes than a light could be dimmed by the closing of a door against it.

Proclus and the Soul's Action

Whatever can be said concerning the soul's actions clearly rests on the assumption that conscious processes require an agent to contain, energize and direct them, and the justification for this will be considered later on. For the present purpose, another way of considering the transcendent nature of the soul can be found where its active powers extend to mathematical operations, as explained by Proclus in the Prologue to his commentary on Euclid. The central issue here is the precision of mathematical reasoning, as instanced by the geometrical properties provable for circles and triangles. The precision of what is proved about them cannot come from any sensorily-perceived circular or triangular objects, because they always fall short of exactitude, and they are in any case always undergoing change, whether rapidly or slowly. Nothing in them is pure and undivided. Besides, the shapes of things perceived in the sense world are also subject to changes resulting from various kinds of perspective distortion.

Theorems, however, relate to ideal figures which are outside change and all variable conditions and, as Proclus puts it, 'whatever yields knowledge that is steadfast has that quality itself in greater degree.'(ibid.) Since this cannot come from any material structures, the only other source must be the soul, which performs the mathematical operations. This is explained on the basis that the Forms are present in the soul, not as they are in their absolute state, and still less as they are in their instantiated state, but in a state or level of being which is partially individualized, though still prior to instantiation. Nevertheless, Proclus does not argue that the soul could be purely and simply an epitome of the Forms. If it were, there would be no ground for the differences between persons, besides which it would allow no basis for the fact that the whole person has a will which is able to work with the Forms according to his or her own scale of priorities. But while soul and body comprise their own equivalents of all instantiated realities, they are governed by a will which defines both the individual and his purposes.

Be that as it may, the important point here is that the soul can project and work with ideas and visual forms which do not depend on sense experience. In the soul they are known under modes which never characterize the material world as such, for example exactitude and universality. These properties of mathematical objects, along with necessity and immutability, confirm their transcendental origin. Totality or universality appears in the way in which a theorem applies to all particular cases. This 'allness' or totality is beyond anything open to sense perception, but here again the soul's nature is conversant with it.

Proclus adds the further consideration that if the originals of things known were the same as the objects in the sense world, the soul would belong to a level of being inferior to that of material objects, since they at least receive the Forms directly. The soul would have no original principles in itself, since its only 'originals' would be the material things in the outside world, for which the soul would have to be a mere reflector. Such a thing could only be said *per impossibile* because, without the soul, we could not know any kind of outside world:

> Soul, then, is the locus of primary, matter of secondary realities; soul the locus of things pre-eminently real, matter of things derivative from them; soul the locus of essential beings, matter of things that come to be by afterthought.[9]

The study of mathematics has thus a spiritual function. Far from

9. Proclus, *A Commentary on the First Book of Euclid's Elements*, Prologue Part I, [12]–[15], Glenn R. Morrow tr. (Princeton: Princeton University Press, 1970).

being concerned only with numbers and geometrical forms for their own sake, these things are studied so that the corresponding properties in the soul, and thereby the soul's transcendental nature, can be made known at the same time. Objects in the sense world awaken the mind, firstly to their Originals, and thence to the presence of those Originals in the soul. Mathematical truths are like fragmentary reflections of our own essential nature, and the way in which they can be increased in number by the study of them reflects the endless productive power of the soul, as well as its primacy over sensibles.

The 'motion' peculiar to the soul is not confined to productive activity, because it also moves immaterially between first principles and conclusions, that is, between the unity and immutability of intellect and the changing and multiple contents of the external world. This shows how the soul is not to be identified with either pure immutability, as would appear from the *Surangama Sutra,* or with the flux of nature, as would appear to common sense, but embraces both extremes. This lies at the heart of the cosmic function of spirituality. It is the realization of the function of uniting the worlds of spirit and matter, by which man is the uniquely necessary bond of union between God and nature. Such is the foundation of the archetypal world-order, under which nature is orderly and benign.

Although this mediating function is a potentiality of the rational soul, it is one which it is under no necessity to realize. Its chosen activity can confine itself to the natural level without any apparent conflict with its own nature, because, paradoxically, it could not feel any such conflict without having some measure of the possibility which it is not in fact realizing. There is thus no simple answer to the question as to whether the personal and individual soul is a spiritual entity or not, since there is a necessarily conditional element here, which will be discussed later. On the other hand, the spirituality and the immortality of the intellectual principle is so far beyond change and contingency that salvation cannot be an issue for it.

To return to the question of agency, this is essential for the soul's substantive nature, since an immaterial substance is being-capable-of-action. If its power of agency was denied, there would remain two possibilities: that agency was a reality in itself, but one which was not relevant here; or that the idea of agency is false or meaningless as such. The latter alternative, assuming one can believe it even for the sake of argument, takes one too far into Humeian scepticism to have any way of engaging with the present subject. But if agency is admitted to be a reality, one must find a rule to decide where agency is necessarily present and where it is not. In the case of random and unintelligent events, there is no difficulty in admitting its absence, but what of cases where intelligence and purpose are manifest? Even the simplest perception is a choice in preference to countless others. In such cases, those who deny agency in the soul must be able to say what conscious processes would be like if agency actually *was* present in them. If they cannot do so, they cannot be supposed to understand the meaning of their declared belief its absence.

Conversely, if those who maintain the necessity for agency have to say what conscious processes would be like *without* an agent, they need only reply that they would consist of meaningless random bits, because entropy only rises, and order does not generate itself. This is why equating 'I see X' with 'There exists a seeing of X' alone is to ignore the whole realm of intelligent purpose; in fact, both Buddhism and modern reductionist philosophy do this. If one starts by denying the presence of agency, there can in any case be no credible answer to the question as to what mental and perceptual processes would be like if agency did enter into them, and this is one reason why the idea that the soul is an agent, and therefore a substance, is not undermined by reductionist arguments.

General Conditions of Transcendence

The soul's transcendence in relation to the body to which it uniquely corresponds can also be seen in the ways in which the proof of any truth can be repeated indefinitely with the same result, regardless of all the changes to which the body is subject. Whether it be a calculation or a deduction, this identical repeatability in the life of one person can equally well be extended beyond the individual to any number of other persons who can prove the same thing for themselves. This clearly applies despite the countless physical differences between the lives of the persons involved. The very fact that we can know the successive acts of verification to be identical in content is itself made possible by a stable identity in the soul which is exempt from natural forces. One knows oneself at this moment to be identical with oneself in the previous moment, and that the self in that previous moment was identical with the one before that, and so on; the changes one undergoes at the same time are only known in the context of this on-going identity.

Even where changes in the body interrupt memories of less essential things, we only have to be reminded of the things forgotten to know them as identical with the original memories we had of them. This shows that where the body has an influence of its own on the mind, the result is the negative one of interrupting and disorganizing, this being the opposite of the correct relationship, which lies rather in action by the soul on the body. Where this action or control is present, things remembered are integrated with the knowledge and memory of one's own continuing identity. Subject to this condition, things known to be true and things known to be untrue cannot change as long as they have the immutability of the same factual basis, or in other words, the true cannot become more or less true, and similarly with the untrue.

Facts of this kind defy forms of thought which deny dualism and treat the person as a 'single subject' or an interactive unity of natural forces. Such thinking would exclude any objective basis for thought being true or false, which would only be possible by convention. This is because the natural forces operating through the brain and the nervous system function just as effectively when we say that seven nines are sixty-two, as when we say they are sixty-three.

Strictly anti-dualistic thinking allows no basic distinction between mental events and any kind of subsistent realities or universals. For the same reason it allows no objective meaning to the distinction between right and wrong. Neither does it allow any meaning to ideas of reference to self or others, or to concepts by which one thing can be 'about' another, because these things require the difference between transcendent and immanent levels of consciousness. Natural forces applied to objects act and react on one another in similar and reciprocal ways, whereas knowledge requires a 'one-way relation' between the cognitive and sensory levels of the personality, that is to say, one which allows an activity by the soul whereby it receives the contents of sensation without being affected by them in its inner operation. While this kind of relation has no parallel on the plane of natural forces, the laws of the latter depend on it for their discovery and application. Such things are direct manifestations of the 'naturally supernatural'.

This by no means excludes the fact that a good deal else of our mental life is caused by processes in our brains and bodies. Mental events originating in this way interact with the intellectual part of the personality and the thoughts it originates in its own way. While sensations must come from physical causes alone, emotions and imaginations may or may not do so, depending on how and where they originate. Emotions and imaginations can just as well be caused by the rational and intellectual powers acting on them in conjunction with sense, as by external natural causes acting on the emotions. Those which originate in this way, that is, in response to ideas, balance and correct those which result from the body's chemistry and outside forces. Without this corrective action, life would be lived on a single level, which in the extreme case would mean that the person was effectively a stimulus-response mechanism, confined to the sense-level.

Although the most essential part of the personality would be thereby excluded, this sense-bound mode of existence would nevertheless meet the criteria of most kinds of anti-dualistic conceptions of the person. This raises the question as to whether belief in single-subject identity is more the cause of a spiritual vacuum than it is the product of one. In either case, it is all too appropriate to an ethos without values. The personal identity it envisages is really a kind of sleep, because when we are asleep, the flow of mental images and feelings is indeed almost wholly the result of natural forces with no conceptual overview. This condition explains why the sinful state is referred to as 'unawakened'. There is no practical reason, however, why such a mode of existence should not be a norm on anti-dualistic principles.

The invasive power of continual change in the body and in its environment is formidable, but this fact only serves to highlight *a contrario* the power of rational consciousness, which can retain its own identity regardless of these things, while at the same time forming objective representations of them. The natural changes in the body alone include changes in its external temperature, the amount of sugars, oxygen and water in the blood, the pulse rate, how near or far one is from times of sleeping, the particular strengths of different emotions and physical needs, and the quantity of cosmic and environmental energy one is subject to.

These are just a small selection of such changing states, each one of which varies in a more or less cyclic manner between certain limits, so that it is impossible for all or even most of them to return to the same level at the same time as any of the others. The natural forces acting in and through the body are constantly forming new combinations which could never recur in one human lifetime. All this is apart from the ageing process, which proceeds irreversibly in the same direction, imposing its own kind of constant change. This process is in turn connected with the fact that the material the body is composed of is constantly wearing away and being re-placed. The body is in effect nothing but change, therefore, and the brain is even more unstable, its structures lasting only a few days, and in some cases only a matter of hours. Identity has no material basis, therefore, and so would not be possible on a monistic or single-subject basis, but only on that of a soul which can transcend change.

This exemption from change in the basic nature of the soul is also an aspect of its being a substance which, when present, gives the body unity and activity, and when no longer there, leaves only inertia and decay. The unity and the individuation of the person thus does not come from the body, but only from an in-forming principle which imposes a measure of unity upon a system of ceaseless change. Similarly, none of the causal powers we possess originates in the body, no matter how necessary the body may be as an instrument and mediator of such powers. It follows from what has been indicated above that if our physical nature alone was our essence and was not combined with another substance which participated in its properties while being of a different nature, we should be devoid of any kind of conscious identity.

The Platonic Idea of Salvation

In view of the difference between the individual soul and the universal ground of consciousness, there can easily be confusion over the question whether the human soul is inherently immortal. As already indicated, immortality can be real in a true but trivial way which confounds it with the immortality of the essence of any consciousness, while on the other hand, for the soul, its true meaning is realized through the prevailing direction of mind and will. In the latter case, it is real in a personal though conditional manner, resulting from a response to grace in which the personality as a whole becomes integrated about the spiritual core of the being which is closest by nature to God. This is where the soul is said to find salvation.

Because this need not be the case, since the process of identification or assimilation can equally well be directed only to the mortal nature, there is more than one meaning for the immortality of the soul. If the body, and what concerns it and its destiny dominate the soul's activity, its separate survival clearly would still be real, but meaningless in terms of its specific possibilities. There would be an insoluble conflict, continued into the afterlife, between an essentially spiritual being and the alien reality it is bound to. In the last analysis, this would mean willing the impossible, that is, an impossible identification.[10]

But if the whole person is 'converted' voluntarily to his inner principle, and the not-necessarily immortal participates in the necessarily immortal, the effect is one of regeneration. This conditional or 'realizational' nature of positive immortality or salvation is summed up by Plato at the end of the *Timaeus* in a way which makes it clear that all this depends on the soul's assimilation to one mode of reality rather than another, when its will is open to the attraction of the truly real. This assimilation derives meaning from the difference between the material or instantial realm and that of the Forms:

10. This conception is adequate to orthodoxy, as it gives a theoretical basis for Hell and Purgatory, and Heaven.

> Now if a man is entirely dedicated to appetites and ambitions and devotes all his energies to these, all his thoughts must needs be mortal, and he cannot help but become altogether mortal (so far as that is possible) since he has fostered the growth of his mortality. If, however, he has set his heart on learning and true wisdom, and has exercised that part of himself above all others, he is surely bound to think thoughts immortal and divine, if he lay hold on truth; nor can he fail to possess immortality in the fullest measure that human nature allows. And inasmuch as he is forever cherishing the divine part and tending the guardian genius that dwells with him in good estate, he must needs be superlatively happy. Now there is one way only of caring for anything, namely, to give it the nourishment and motion proper to it. The motions akin to the divine part in us are the thoughts and revolutions of the universe; these therefore every man should follow, and correcting those circuits in the head that were deranged at birth, by learning to recognize the harmonies and revolutions of the world, he should bring the intelligent part, according to its pristine nature, unto the likeness of that which intelligence discerns, and thereby achieve the best life set by the gods before mankind both for this present time and for the time to come.[11]

This is possibly the most humanly accessible account of what is involved in salvation, and the fact that this idea of salvation is suited to culturally superior individuals who perceive the higher possibilities of the intellect ought not to blind anyone to the fact that it is also suited to all kinds of people who are sincerely willing to learn the spiritual lessons of whatever kind of life they have to live. Innumerable good persons with no theoretical knowledge of what is involved in this nevertheless follow it by a kind of instinct. Because of this, the Platonic idea of salvation must be the most universal on a natural level; because of its simplicity, it necessarily forms part of all other and more complex means of salvation, whether they recog-

11. *Timaeus* 90 B–D, John Warrington translation (London: J.M. Dent & Sons Ltd., 1965).

nize it or not. Should the validity of this 'common factor' in all religions be denied, moreover, there would be no logical alternative to a religious exclusivism which must deny the possibility of salvation to all who were outside a given religion. That is in fact the form which religious belief frequently took in times when faith was still strong and when the esoteric was hidden.

Where this possibility is admitted in orthodox exoteric belief, it is regarded as something purely ancillary to the means derived from revelation, and it is so by definition in any such context. However, it is at least theoretically possible to invert this relationship, to the effect that the ways of revealed religion were ancillary to the Platonic way, that is, to what Plato meant by 'conversion'.[12] Pure logic allows this, even though normal religious intuition does not, and the fact that such a result is conceivable is enough to show that revealed ways which teach salvation do not have to be closed systems in order to be necessary as sources of grace. Though most of the great religions would deny this point of view, it involves a conception which allows an 'Archimedean point' from whence revealed forms of salvation *from* evil could be the condition for a salvation *for a* certain kind of activity, a distinction drawn by Berdyaev, but by very few others. If, then, the ideal of sainthood was inclusive of the intellectually authentic individual, it would, to say the least, be a distinct advance on the mundane purposes with which the religious ideal is identified today.

While the effectiveness of this 'assimilative conversion' way of salvation is very hard to evaluate in the abstract, because neither it nor revealed religion ever operate wholly without the other, one factor in its favour is its independence of any particular kinds of relation between the individual and the outside world as he knows it in his personal world-representation. At the same time, it also means that objections to 'intellectualism' are not necessarily spiritually relevant, because everything depends on how far the intellectualism is a vital commitment. It works in a dimension of the self which is not solely

12. See *Republic* bk. VII: 518D, 521C, 525C, 533D, Paul Shorey, tr., *The Collected Works of Plato* (Princeton: Princeton University Press, 1973).

a *relatum* among externals like the ego, but is the soul-microcosm which is the counterpart to the self of common sense.

In this dimension, the ego and its outer relations reside as contents, and this is why the soul is not subject to the same kind of relations as the ego. Its relations are to God and to other spirits, which are seldom understood with the clarity with which the ego's relations to the external world of the collectivity are understood. The real self contains the interaction of these inner and outer modes of being, and the proportions between ego-life and soul-life vary endlessly from one person to another. Thus autonomy and spiritual dependence are always finely mingled, and in ways which are unique to the individual.

Where this truth is ignored, and persons are equated with their egos alone, the result can only be a reduction of religion to forms of social behavior, which is an extreme position, the opposite of which is the purely soul-centered perspective of New Age religion. There is a 'spiritual law of gravity', so to speak, which always inclines people to one or the other of two opposite kinds of false limitation, one of which would be a warrant for persecution, and the other a cult of pure subjectivity. The resolution of such oppositions is not hard to see in the light of the assimilative principle: though its work is not self-sufficient, the intellect comprises both the Way and the Destination, and through it man can be taught by God. This possibility is ignored by modern teachers of the esoteric almost as much as by those of the exoteric.

Love and Knowledge

In case the Platonic idea of salvation should still appear to depend on a belief that the intellect is the highest reality to which we have any access, the fact remains that for both Christianity and Platonism the divinity above intellect is an essential presence. For Christianity, this presence is manifest in the form of love or charity, which can pervade all activity, not least the intellectual kind, a conclusion which was resisted by Guénon on the grounds that it would adulterate the content of the pure intelligence, and so detract from its certainty. He took this kind of intellectualist position because he thought of charity as something on the same level as that of the intellect, and so liable to compete with it. In reality, no such confusion is possible, because the highest principle relates to subordinate realities, not as an alien force, but by containing them and uniting them with their eternal values. Love is the highest expression of the will, and in any case, the intellect is never independent of the will of the individual person, and still less of the will of God.

Where the personal relationship to God is concerned, the kind of life described by Plato in the above quotation would not be possible without a love of God which was strong enough to subordinate other loves, and which was the conscious counterpart for God's love of the creature, even where the personal nature of God is not fully understood. This is also a love which overflows the boundaries of the personal and the non-personal, and which recognizes that truth as truth has its rights. The full development of the immortal nature is implicitly also a realization of a partial community of nature with God, in Whom there is both personality and impersonality. The work of the intellect at the center of the personality involves all parts of the latter, such that all are integrated about the same center. This is poles apart from a supposed salvation of the intellectual principle alone, deliberately out of relation to the rest of the self which has an actual need for it.

Despite the difference between this and the Non-Dualist idea of salvation, there are also teachings in Western tradition which suggest that this is not so much a relationship as an actual replacement of the soul or psychic self with God. This, however, is a devotional expression, and not one of theoretical principles because, taken literally, it would mean that God too was just a psychic individual, besides which it would break up the order of being by confounding beings which belong to very different places in it, which of course means pantheism. If, on the other hand, the psychic individual was replaced by a God who was *not a* being of this kind, it could only mean the sudden disappearance of the person concerned.

Unlike the self-realization as *Nous* or *Atman,* the assimilative conception of salvation is a process of transformation in which the naturally unspiritual becomes spiritual by collaboration with a divine inspiration which involves the whole being, acting between soul and spirit and between body and spirit by means of the soul. Far from being just an enclosed equation of truth-with-truth, this means a real increase in the created good which enriches the world on all the levels of being in which the human state participates.

Since personality typifies what we most clearly are, its presence in any idea of salvation is necessary if this idea is to be meaningful. Those who reject this idea do so in the belief that personality is limited of itself, and not just accidentally. This also involves the assumption that of the primal pair, the Limit and the Infinite, only the Infinite is real, as though it were not relative to the other principle. If, as appears to be the case, personhood is capable of being enlarged without limit in proportion to its spiritual development, while retaining its specific personal nature, such objections to it would be circumvented.

While it may be said that the monistic conception of salvation comprises incomparably more than words alone can convey, it should be remembered that the same could be said for the personal conception as well. In geometrical terms, the difference between the personal and non-personal conceptions is like that between a cross and a circle, that is, between a center which radiates outward so as to relate countless other realities to itself, and a center in a sealed enclosure. Given the range of development of which the soul is capable, the Incarnation is not merely an inspirational example leading to an impersonal goal, but rather both the Incarnation and personhood have an intrinsic meaning which continues through this world into eternity.

8

Conditions For Mystical Union

The Problem of Definition

It is generally agreed that the union of the soul with God is the goal of religion, and that its highest forms are the subject of mystical writings, but there is far less agreement about the exact nature of this union. For theistic and dualistic[1] mystical experience, it is a union between real persons, whereas from a monistic perspective, such union means a reduction of different beings to God alone. Before we can judge between these positions, we need to be able to understand why it should be possible for created or finite beings to be capable of any kind of union with God. Union is by definition only possible between similars, not between things which differ absolutely, and in the present case, the difference between God and a creature is more extreme than between any two finite entities.

A simplistic way of answering this problem would be to say that union means the final disappearance of whatever it is that differs from God in the relationship. This, however, is merely a denial of the real problem, because on this basis, union *qua* union would be voided of content. God is by definition not passive to any action from other beings, however, so mystical union could not be imposed

1. This does *not* refer to the Gnostic dualism between God and a purely evil material world. It is rather a dualistic theory of knowledge, applied to relations between real persons who are not reducible to a single entity. Non-Dualism may appear to concede something to the dualistic position, but it inclines too closely to Monism for this to be effectual.

on God from without, that is, by a created being. If therefore, such union is a reality, by what means could the gulf between creature and Creator be bridged? The answer to this can be found from an application of two principles, which are often taken as presuppositions by those who use them. These are, firstly, the Principle of Plenitude, and secondly the principle that the unity of the world means that the Whole is present in every part. The latter is usually expressed in the idea that man is a microcosm of his world. The first of these two principles is firstly a part of Neoplatonic tradition, and then of Christian tradition, via the Pseudo-Areopagite, with the hierarchy of angels. Archangels, Powers, Principalities, Dominions, Thrones, Cherubim, and Seraphim.

If these principles are provisionally accepted for the present purpose, we can simply consider the implication of Plenitude, that every possibility of being, from that most proximate to God, down to that remotest by nature from God, must be represented by actual beings. All possibilities of being will be realized. If, besides, man is a microcosm of all being, it will follow that there must be an element in his being which corresponds by nature to God, as well as elements or possibilities corresponding to all other levels of being. This divine part of the soul could not be God as such, even though it must share many or most of the divine attributes, because this would mean that God as such could be instanced in particulars, like the Form of a figure or quality. This would exclude God's transcendence and make nature divine. Nevertheless, the complete scale of creation must include something which is Divine without being God, rather in the way that reason, say, is human without actually being man. Of such a nature is the attribute which forms the continuity between God and man, on which the possibility of spiritual union between them depends.

Many minds misunderstand the idea that all levels of being must be actualized. From an empirical point of view, the discontinuities between the kinds of being which exist on this earth are all too apparent. But in regard to all times and all parts of space without restriction, all the separate incomplete instances of being add up to a complete whole. This idea that all levels of being are realized follows from the causal law according to which a productive cause must first produce what is most like itself, and subsequently things increasingly less like it. This idea excludes gaps in the universal sequence, since each level derives from the one adjacent to it. If, in addition to the First Cause, each subsequent state of being was also a co-cause of the ones subsequent to it, then continuity throughout the series would be necessary in order that the causal action of the Highest should be able to advance to its term unchecked. If in fact some of the possible orders of being were universally excluded, this would do harm to the ones which did exist. An incomplete scale of being would aggravate the differences between the kinds of being by depriving them of mediators and so weakening the relationships between them. This would increase the possibilities of conflict and violence among all beings, and the world could not be morally as good as it would be if all kinds existed. Some evils would result from the world's very constitution, which would be opposed to what is believed about the Creator.

To make a slight digression, this might seem to imply that man should be the co-cause of the natural world after God, whereas man is the last being to be created in *Genesis*, in a way seemingly opposed to the above idea of causation. However, what is first created and most like God is the world in its pristine state. Man is in some sense the 'last' part of it if we think temporally, because the essential nature of man can only be realized in fully corresponding to the whole of creation, which must necessarily exist as man's precondition.

The creation of mankind last of all is thus in accordance with the way in which the created world is like an inverted reflection of its eternal causes, with the 'first' coming 'last', and vice-versa. Although mankind belongs to the highest order of creation according to its archetypal Form, its creative power is incomparably less on the level where it is instantiated in matter, at the lower end of the realm of spirits.

The Testimony of Mysticism

The continuum or 'great chain' of being can be seen in the functioning of most things in the material world, from organisms to artefacts. For all such entities, the time for which it exists is a continuum running from its fullest physical order to its final expended state, following the principle that every cause produces first what is most like itself. In such sequences, arbitrary voids would destroy the coherence of the world, and make it opaque to man's understanding, breaking the harmony of the inner and outer realities of mind and matter. Such is the view of the continuum of being on the universal scale from which it would follow that there is a part of the soul which is congruent with divinity. I have referred to this principle, which is equally natural and supernatural, elsewhere as the Philosophers' Stone, which is prior to all else that we know as creation. It is a reality common to the human spirit and the Spirit of God, participating in both the divine and human natures.

It must be said, by the way, that there are consequences here for the way in which we understand the Fall. Since the Fall did not mean that man lost the divine spark—or else he would have become an animal—it would rather mean that his individual created nature was no longer integrated with its spiritual center. In addition, his ability to re-establish the lost inner harmony by his own efforts alone was either greatly weakened or lost altogether. But despite the consequent corruption of human nature, the divine spark was not affected in itself, but only in its relation to the personality. However, grace is always able to reactivate it, and thus it makes possible a spiritual and mystically effectual function for human intelligence, in regard to which it is said in the *Hermetica* that 'soul is in body, mind is in soul, and God [*theos*] is in mind,'[2] for which reason, the intellect is traditionally considered as the most direct means of relating to God and the supernatural.

But if there is such a reality residing in the human soul, the idea of the microcosm must require that there be a corresponding reality in the macrocosmic order. What might that be? An answer can be found in Hans Martensen' s account of Jacob Boehme's vision of the Eternal Sophia.[3] Coming fourth in order after the three Persons of

2. *Hermetica*, bk. XII, I, Walter Scott tr. (Bath, UK: Solos Press, 1992), p95. In ancient Greek texts *theos* was more vague than in Christian texts, and signified simply 'the divine'.

3. Hans L. Martensen, *Jacob Boehme*, Steven Hobhouse, ed., T. Rhys Evans, tr. (London: Rockliff Press, nd.), pp107–108.

the Trinity, is the Uncreated Heaven, which is an objectivized self-projection of God, resulting from God's self-knowledge under the form of multiplicity. It is said to proceed from the Father and to be 'gathered by the Son into an intellectual unity' and is 'shaped by the Spirit into a world of ideas, different from God, and yet inseparable from him.'[4]

This is also said to coincide with the Platonic realm of Forms, being the impersonal and objective side of the Glory of God. This quasi-divine reality is the condition for beauty in God, because without it God would be solely a pure spirit, that is, solely a being of thinking, knowing and willing, and not also 'imagining, image-forming, figure-shaping.'

> This thing, which is essentially and incessantly energized, is the impersonal Glory of God, the objectivity that encircles Him, and is at once an ideal world and a natural world in ideal beauty. It is God's Uncreated Heaven ... the imperishable garment of light which God eternally produces.[5]

Those who suppose that the objective reality of the Forms is a narrowly Platonic issue should be aware that the majority of the great mystics are agreed that there are in effect three worlds, the world of natural experience, the world of Forms or essences, and the super-essential world of God as such.[6] It is in the first of these three worlds that the soul practises Conversion, in the second, Illumination, and in the third, Union. The near-unanimity among the mystics about this shows that Plato was a true mystic who was also a philosopher. The 'divine spark' or 'eye of the soul' would thus be of one and the same nature as the objective Glory of God, or Eternal Sophia.

A Biblical text which would confirm this conception of the human soul is to be found in Ecclesiastes 3:11: 'also he has put eternity into man's mind, yet so that he cannot find out what God has

4. Ibid., pt. II, chap. v.

5. Ibid., p108.

6. Evelyn Underhill, *The Essentials of Mysticism*, first essay (London: J.M. Dent & Sons, 1920).

done from the beginning to the end.' In the Septuagint, this eternity is written as *sympanta ton aiona* or 'the whole eternity' for greater emphasis. The share in divinity which this implies does not suffice for man to be able to read God's purposes, except in limited ways, which are in keeping with the idea that this share is divine, but not God as such. Since 'eternity' and 'world' are the same word (*aion*) in Greek, this idea corresponds exactly with the idea of man as microcosm.[7] The above text should also be related to 'He put his own light in their hearts to show them the magnificence of his works' (Eccl. 7:8).

Neoplatonism and Mystical Union

The kind of union between man and God which can exist on this basis is also unmistakably that of the Neoplatonic tradition, which combines the qualities of a theistic form of mysticism with an extensive theoretical account of the states involved. This can be seen from the fact that union of the soul with God does not mean a literal identification, according to both Proclus or Plotinus. Instead, they are assumed to remain separate substances, so that the functions of abiding in, proceeding from, and union with, or 'conversion' (*epistrophe*) to God are understood to go on continuously, since all three are essential functions of each substance. As A.C. Lloyd expresses it, 'remaining, proceeding, and reverting are all different but inseparable—all parts of a timeless movement.'[8]

This manner of union is an essential factor in prayer and worship, and it is effected by something analogous to physical contact

7. Most modern translations deliberately obscure this point. In the *Jerusalem Bible*, this text is rendered: 'he has permitted man to consider time in its wholeness.' In the *Catholic New R.S.V.* it says: 'he has put a sense of past and future into their minds.' In the *NEB* it says that God has 'given man a sense of time, past and future.' In the *Good News Bible*, it actually says that God has 'given man a desire to know the future.' This is an example of the way in which the metaphysical content of religion is being suppressed by its modern custodians. Some honorable but less influential exceptions include the ordinary *Catholic RSV*, *The New International Bible*, and the *New American Standard Bible*.

8. *The Anatomy of Neoplatonism*, chap. 5, p130 (Oxford, 1991).

rather than vision, because without this there would not be a full continuum of being:

> contact is necessary, according to which we touch the divine essence with the summit of our soul, and this mode of union has the effect of establishing *the one* of the soul in *The One* of the Gods, and causing our energy to become one with the divine energy; according to which we are no longer ourselves, but are absorbed as it were in the Gods. . . .[9]

This union is conceived as a fusion of energies rather than a fusion of identities, because the latter would only be possible if spiritual substances acted in the same way as do material ones, which necessarily lose identity in mingling. This directly involves only the highest part of the soul. In the ethos of ancient philosophy this point would be taken for granted. Spiritual substances are in a sense at an opposite pole from material substances, because the former relate to one another by mutual inclusion, whereas the latter relate to one another by mutual exclusion: e.g., *qua* souls we include one another, and *qua* bodies we exclude one another. Only in the case of mutual exclusion could there be any question of a mingling that would eliminate the identities which were the subjects of the union.

A consequence of this conception is that the union or conversion of the highest part of the soul to divinity follows from the same kind of act as its own self-conversion. This is because it is understood that the microcosm implies that man's concentration on the spiritual center of his own being will involve a concentration on the Center of all beings, rather as the center of a circle communicates with the axis which passes through that center at right angles to the plane of the circle. In Plotinus' terms, 'Intellect must be intent upon its Prior; its introversion is a conversion upon the Principle.'[10]

If, however, the conversion or mystical union follows the procession of the individual being from his source, will it not obliterate the identity which has been realized by this procession? In fact,

9. Proclus, *Commentary on the Timaeus,* 1211c (Frome, UK: The Prometheus Trust, 1998), p198, Thomas Taylor translation.

10. *Enneads*, VI, 9, 2. MacKenna translation.

conversion or reversion, (*epistrophe*),[11] does not mean a simple cancellation of the procession, so much as a counter-tension or inclination, rather as an orbiting body has a tension towards the body it revolves around. Abiding, proceeding and reverting are related to Being, Life, and Knowledge respectively. Animals receive being and life, but their life is solely one of 'procession'. They do not have reversion, whence their life diverges continuously from its source until it dissolves.

Only the power of reversion can balance procession and liberate the being from the entropic current of time. In other words, procession alone ultimately negates itself, whereas reversion preserves it. What reverts is something far more complex than what originally proceeded, and for that reason alone it is not a negation of what went before. In this connection, Proclus speaks of 'a divinely inspired energy of the soul, converting herself to herself and to divinity, perceiving the causes of all things in the gods.'[12]

In the same text, he says that divinity produces our essence, thereby giving us '*a self-motive nature ordered to the choice of the good*' (my italics).[13] This agrees with Augustine's teaching that part of the essence of the soul is an image of the Trinity comprising being, knowledge, and love of being and knowing. The condition for mystical union is partly the same as for knowledge, according to which only like can know like, expressed by Proclus in a fourfold division recalling Plato's Divided Line:

> For all things are known by the similar, that which is sensible by sense, that which is the object of science by science, that which is intelligible by intellect, and that which is one by that which is characterized by unity.[14]

The highest unity in the soul communes with the highest unity

11. For the use of this word see Proclus, *Elements of Theology*, props. 31 and 32, E. R. Dodds, ed.

12. *Commentary on the Timaeus* vol. 1, 1215c, p201,Thomas Taylor translation, from 1816 edition.

13. Ibid., 1216, p202.

14. *On Providence and Fate*, §24, Thomas Taylor translation, from 1816 edition of *The Theology of Plato*.

among all beings, in a way which transcends the distinction of subject and object. While this means a level of unity above that of knowledge as such, it is an entry into the center of things from whence all levels of knowledge radiate. This view of unitive knowledge is also common to Plotinus (IV, 8, 4), where he describes the soul's tension between 'the life here' and 'the life There'. By dwelling in union with the Universal Soul, one participates in the universal rulership of the world.

On the other hand, the negative possibilities of procession can prevail against this when it excludes reversion. In this case, souls grow focused upon themselves, rather than upon the reality which sustains them. This withdrawal into self produces a scattering of those affected by it, and the resulting spiritual isolation means a weakening and a loss of options, as might be expected of a process of contraction. This includes a concentration on the body and the body's concerns, and, following the body's property of exclusion, it leads to a war of all against all. Those so affected are fated to struggle ever harder with ever less effect, because they are no longer joined to the source of being and power.

This is not to say that procession is an evil in itself, since none of the primal realities is evil, and it is in any case necessary for all beings to achieve their full development and individuation. But when it takes the form referred to by Plotinus, where it assumes the dominance natural for it in the animal kingdom, the individual perversely identifies with it alone. Thus the function of life and growth denies its ultimate destiny. The opposite of this condition, i.e., reversion, results in a free union between two real beings:

> This conversion brings gain: at the first stage, that of separation, a man is aware of self; but retreating inwards, he becomes the possessor of all; he puts sense away behind him in dread of the separated life and becomes one in the Divine; if he plans to see in separation, he sets himself outside.[15]

Union does not limit the options of free will, therefore, but rather expands them, so that vision can be had on widely-different levels.

15. *Enneads*, V, 8, 11.

Plotinus' conception of mystical union can be seen to be dualistic in other texts as well:

> Souls that take this way (of ascent) have a place in both spheres, living of necessity the life There and the life here by turns, the upper life reigning in those able to consort more continuously with the divine Intellect. . . .[16]

It appears that the lower functions of the soul remain alongside the union of its highest part with the One. Thus it is not a question of one part of the soul being real and the rest illusory. Even in its non-mystical states, the soul in all individuals is like a bridge connecting three levels of reality, whether they have any conscious interest in this function or not:

> even our human soul has not sunk entire; something of it is continuously in the Intellectual realm. . . .[17]

The keynote of this conception is a multi-layered consciousness, the parts of which function simultaneously. Significantly, Plotinus does not speak of substantive self-identification with the One, the *Nous*, or the World Soul, which would follow if the highest part of the soul literally was God. For Neoplatonism, the One is no more identified with the whole of reality than God is in Christian theology. This is why union with the One is not conceived in the manner of a pantheistic union. Since the One is the same as the Good, moreover, the categories of virtue and vice cannot be spiritually transcended, as they are in pantheistic systems. Here again, there is a clear alignment between Christianity and Neoplatonism.

Plotinus speaks of union for the most part in tactile terms, in order to emphasize the resulting unity, rather than in terms of vision, which is oriented towards duality, since it requires the parties to be clearly external to one another. It is therefore so much the more significant that he does not see this union as one of the pantheistic kind, but rather as a union between the center of the 'little world' and that of the 'great world'. Not surprisingly, then, it is

16. *Enneads*, IV, 8, 4.
17. *Enneads*, IV, 8, 8.

never suggested that either the soul itself, or its 'center' or 'summit', is one and the same as the One or the *Nous*, no matter how closely related they may be.

Christian mystics have discovered the same kind of relation-in-union for themselves. Even if one makes allowances for the way in which they have interpreted their experiences in Neoplatonic terms, interpretation cannot create this kind of experience itself. One way in which they differ from the Neoplatonists, however, appears in the way they explain their attraction to God in terms of the action of divine grace, whereas for the Neoplatonists the unitive movement is owing only to the soul's activity, not that of the One, which they believe never takes any notice of any other being.

The Neoplatonists could be justified within certain limits on this point by the existence of the 'divine spark', which is not intrinsically subject to the Fall, and which is essentially 'ordered to the choice of the good.' But on the other hand, they clearly have a defective idea of God, since no kind of oblivion, like that of ignorance of his own creatures, can subsist along with absolute perfection.

In Christian terms, the answer is found in the Trinity, which combines the 'supreme' and 'non-supreme' aspects of God in an overall unity, whereas there is no substantive unity between the One and the *Nous*. The mutuality of attraction and love between God and man would therefore result from a more complete idea of God. Differences over the question of dependence on grace, however, are mostly owing to an exoteric idea of the soul, for which it is purely and simply a fallen creature. A complete idea of union implies activity by both God and man, if 'man' includes his divine principle.

There is another and related difference which can be explained in much the same way, and that is the Plotinian idea that the One does not love those it produces and attracts. The kind of love it is supposed to inspire is therefore of the kind most people find in the love of nature. To love what cannot love in return is certainly a part of love's possibilities, but it is too incomplete to belong to the highest part of them. Here again, the Trinitarian and personal idea of God provides the answer. But Plotinus is consistent with his limited idea of God here, inasmuch he treats nescience as being also a positive quality in human beings, at least as long as they are contemplating the higher realities. The alternative to this, that of admitting inherent limitations to human minds, even the greatest, such that they can only focus on one thing at a time, was felt by Plotinus to be an obstacle to his idea of man's spiritual possibilities.

If therefore nescience of relative things was not to be taken for a limitation in man, neither would it be in God or the One. But this is to ignore the fact that there is no *logical* reason why a being should not be conscious in eternity and time at once; man's disability in this respect is simply a brute fact, which no doubt results from his being a creature, and so cannot imply any equivalent of it in God. This is supported by the *Theologia Germanica*, where it affirms that Christ's divinity meant that in Him, the 'eye of time' and the 'eye of eternity' were always open simultaneously, whereas for human beings, one of them must always close when the other opens.[18]

Relevance to Christian Teachings

This view of mysticism may seem too general by nature to form part of Christian teachings, because in its Plotinian form, it does not indicate any role for love of the creature by the Creator. This view could well appear to follow from Plotinus' self-absorbed conception of the Godhead, which is much the same as that of Aristotle. However, this does not logically exclude the Christian perspective, because the Plotinian account can easily be seen to be the *modus operandi* of a creative act which was inspired by a love for created beings who were foreknown and foreintended as parts of a universal benign purpose.

However central a place we give to a design which consists in God's love of individual creatures for their own sake, there still remains the need to explain how this design is actually effected. Such things cannot be made theoretically intelligible unless we focus on the impersonal structure of creation, as Plotinus does. While intelligibles are impersonal universals, this is balanced by the fact that the divine unity which transcends the human intellect consists of both

18. *Theologia Germanica*, chap. VII, Susanna Winkworth, tr. (London: Macmillan & Co., 1874).

the divine love and the divine intellect, as much for Neoplatonism as for Christianity.

Nevertheless, the mediating role of the 'summit' of the soul, for all its solidarity with theistic religion and mysticism, may still appear to be a metaphysical substitute for the mediating role of Christ between God and man. It was, after all, a part of pagan spirituality. In reality, this is a false opposition, because Christ is the Incarnation of precisely this reality, which is present in all rational beings as 'the true light which enlightens every man' (John 1:9).

One consequence of this is that in all orthodox worship of Christ, the direction of the heart to God entails a parallel direction toward the 'light' or 'divine spark' in oneself at the same time. This spiritual activity is clearly related to the way in which the concentration on self-unity produces an equivalent concentration on the divine unity, referred to previously. A personal relation to God results from this in either case, but with the difference that in the former it is by means of the divine presence in the essence of the soul, while in the latter it is by means of this presence in the external world as a result of revelation. The Incarnation, and the tradition following from it therefore creates in the macrocosm an external equivalent of a conscious primacy of the spiritual center in the microcosm. In practice, if not in principle, interior devotion is always a consequence of exterior revelation, because an effective awareness of supersensible reality is impossible in the long run unless the invisible is 'incarnated' in the visible world.

Because of Christ's Incarnation and its self-propagation through the Church in history, Christian revelation proceeds from something essential to all religion. Its outward and visible form both symbolizes and makes effectual the spiritualization of the soul and the whole person.This is owing to the fact that the life of Christ is a universal model of the being who finds salvation. The celebration of its main events awakens their equivalents in oneself.

But though we depend on the senses for our relation to revelation, this does not imply any corresponding dependence in regard to knowledge, even though it needs to be quickened in the human spirit by this means. We do not derive knowledge from the senses as such, as the exoteric position assumes. In reality, empirical conditions have only an *ad hoc* role here, which is necessary but far from sufficient, because the grace of revelation brings to life something which is part of our essential being and which can become self-verifying when once made conscious.

Even when this intellectual aspect of the faith is not grasped consciously, it is still effective, but in an incomplete manner. The relations between the metaphysical and devotional sides of religion are as free and non-exclusive as those between the macrocosm and the microcosm themselves. The conception of the 'divine spark' as the highest part of the human soul is the basis of the deepest difference between theistic and pantheistic mysticism. Such an element in man is as it were the capstone of a continuous hierarchy of being below God, whereas for pantheism there cannot meaningfully be any such hierarchy, if it is to link actual beings to God. This is because its position depends on there being an illusory distribution of God among innumerable beings, by whom God is disguised. Such beings can still be ordered in a hierarchy, but not in a spiritually effectual manner, since their inherent differences in value and reality are neutralized by being supposedly mere appearances.

If what is not God is not created by God's own will, but results only from emanations, no amount of other attributes can give it any meaning, and even if some monistic thinkers admit the reality of the Great Chain of Being, it can only be in a way which deprives it of any practical function as a support for the created being's relation to God. While this order is believed in universally, its emphasis on the positive aspect of differences between beings must mean that it cannot be truly integrated with doctrines of a monistic or non-dualistic kind. Those who see the latter doctrines as the key to traditional wisdom as a whole will find this to be an objection to their belief, and one which is too often ignored. This would at the same time explain why Monism should have become prevalent in the modern world, where traditional ideas of order and hierarchy have disintegrated on the cultural plane. An essentially profane world is an ideal subject for a metaphysics for which the phenomenal world is illusory.

Moreover, the monistic or non-dualistic position is, however unintentionally, well adapted to the demand of modern people for quick, neat answers to matters of principle. The union of the soul with God according to the principle outlined here, could not be so simplified unless one had the right to say that the soul and God were not really different. In a similar way, all the difficult questions which arise because our world is our representation of objective reality could be simplified away if we had the right to say that this just meant that everything was an illusion. For this reason, the prevalent New Age forms of spiritual enlightenment can be understood as a mutilated and vulgarized Platonism.

If the word 'union' really means union, the idea of mystical union can only be problem-free in terms of theistic and dualistic principles, whether Christian or Neoplatonic. One cannot coherently speak of 'union' if it means the suppression of one of the 'uniands'. It has been claimed by some exponents of Monism that all mystical experience confirms the absolute unity of ultimate reality. They add to this the consequent claim that where such experience is reported in dualistic terms, it can only be because those concerned have allowed the intrusion of cultural and theological prejudices into the interpretation of their experiences.

However, in the light of the foregoing, this argument can reasonably be countered by the claim that supposed monistic experience was a misinterpretation of dualistic experience. If the ultimate reality is pure unity, there must be a mind to know it to be so, and that means something more than the pure unity. At the same time yet other minds can know the mind that knows the Unity, as though reality had a self-multiplying infinite regress in it. This is closely attached to the fact that all mystical states, monistic or dualistic, include the continuation of the subordinate faculties in the same personal life. The dualistic conception makes this easier to understand than does the monistic one, and the principles on which it is based account for the existence and truth of Theistic religion as distinct from Pantheistic.

9

Life, Death, and Resurrection

The Body's Role in Identity

This is a subject that naturally combines a number of issues concerning the Christian tradition, and the relation of its doctrines to the ancient wisdom, as well as the way in which the duality of soul and body should be understood. For modern man, the literal belief in bodily resurrection is one of the most problematic of traditional beliefs, because it appears to be challenged by scientific knowledge, while both its metaphysical basis and its relation to spiritual ideas of immortality are obscure. It involves an idea of the body's role in the personality which is distinctively Christian when compared with the other kinds of beliefs which prevailed in the early centuries AD.

That soul and body form a real duality can be seen from the fact that the body continues to exist unchanged for some time after death. In the special case of those bodies of saints which have remained incorrupt, this can be an indefinite length of time. If non-dualistic theories of human nature were right, on the other hand, the moment of death would have to mean an instantaneous dissolution of the body at the same time. It is therefore pointless to maintain that the soul cannot be separable from the body when the body can exist without the soul. Such basic facts are often resisted out of a fear that they may be a warrant for a return to pre-Christian kinds of spirituality or 'angelism', which depend on a Dualism which is taken so far as to make the relation of soul and body to be merely accidental.

There is in fact a considerable amount of traditional belief that the soul's embodiment is a mere accident to it, a state from whence it must extricate itself so as to prepare for a purely disincarnate state after death. Thus perfection would depend on separation from the body and from any remnant of individuality. For this reason it could be said that pagan spirituality is simple in that it requires only a reversal of our natural condition. In other words, an exclusive self-identification with the body and its conditions is exchanged for an equally exclusive identification with the soul. This is usually understood as a soul undetermined by the unique personality which is manifested by the body.

From a Christian point of view, this option of spiritual paganism is as wide of the mark as its opposite, materialism, because they both ignore what it perceives to be the true nature of man. The latter affirms the reality of persons, while denying them any prospect of salvation, and the former affirms salvation while denying that there is any real person to be saved. The ease with which some individuals can pass to and fro between these options is a good indication that they are both really natural conditions, and therefore two-dimensional, so to speak, in relation to the spirit.

Instead of attributing certain moral evils to the natural involvement with the body as such, Christian tradition has always seen them as a misunderstanding of the soul's relation to the body. This more subtle position is based on the idea that man is by his very essence created as a union of all levels of being and reality. This implies that if man were to be disincarnate, and so purely spiritual in the narrowly literal sense of the word, he would in reality be less perfect in his own kind. He would thus become less like God, not more. This is because God is complete and perfect *qua* pure spirit, whence the only kind of being which can be adequate in its own way to God is one which is also complete and perfect in its own way.

In this connection, Joseph Pieper quotes Aquinas where he says that 'the soul united to the body is more like God because it possesses its own nature more perfectly.'[1] The union of mineral, vegetable, animal, and spiritual modes of being in man is thus what

1. *Leisure the Basis of Culture* (London: Faber & Faber, 1952), pp120–121.

constitutes his 'spiritual species'. But while this idea supports the belief in a necessity for a restoration of the body in the Resurrection, it does not help with modern man's problem that the traditional form of this belief made it out to mean a restoration of the selfsame materials as those by which it is composed here and now. Modern science appears to exclude this, because it can be shown that the composition of the body is in constant change. It can hardly be called 'a' body at all. Every cell of it is ingested from the bodies of plants and animals, so that every one of its cells is either being incorporated or on the way to being replaced by others. We have in effect innumerable bodies in a lifetime.

Through all these changes, the form of the body remains, while its material content comes and goes. These facts would indicate that the resurrected body should be composed of a material quite different from what it had during this life, while retaining the same form, as it did during this life. When this variant on the doctrine was not considered, it gave rise to grotesque problems as to the resurrected state of cannibals and those whom they had eaten. If these problems were not enough, there is also the problem from the traditional point of view that the Resurrection is believed to depend solely on scriptural texts, and not on metaphysical knowledge. The main metaphysical systems seem to allow only a disincarnate and more or less impersonal immortality which does not harmonize with bodily resurrection.

A Physical Aspect of Immortality

This, then, leaves us with two quite different perspectives on immortality and spiritual realization, whose relation needs to be shown to be coherent. What I shall try to show is that this conflict can be overcome by an idea of our destiny which transcends the values of both materialists and spiritualists, while not denying the basic concerns of either. An essential key to this riddle is to be found in a Hermetic teaching which Maurice Nicoll makes extensive use of, and which he quotes as follows:

> think that you are not yet begotten, that you are in the womb, that you are young, that you are old, that you have died, that you

are in the world beyond the grave; grasp in your thought all this at once, all times and places, all substances and magnitudes together; then you can apprehend God.[2]

So far from being an escape into fantasy, this universalized form of identity integrates our individual natures with a world of objective realities, so as to make us able to come up to the measure of what it is to be an image of God. While it is not an alternative to our natural identity, it is a necessary supplement to it. Thus the objective justification for this greater sense of identity depends on the fact that all our previous states of being still *really exist* in objective reality, even though they are not perceptible by our time-bound senses. Sense is necessarily tied to the present moment, and that is why it is always deceptive if taken for anything like a complete representation of reality.

The illusion of temporality can be overcome when we perceive the passage of time as a movement through a fourth dimension. In this dimension there are no distinctions of past, present, and future. One and the same object goes from being future to being present, and from being present to being past, as long as our awareness is confined to the three dimensions of space at any moment in time. However, the object is not changed in itself, as the only real change is owing to the movement of our consciousness. Absolute change is in any case a contradiction, since change always has to be relative to something which does not change.

Suppose an object is at a certain spatial position at time T1. It can only cease to be in that spatial position at a later time T2, because any denial that it retained its place at T1 would involve a denial of the law of non-contradiction; the combination of space-time data, once made, is immutable. Our perception of an object which we perceive to remain unchanged is always confined to what can be perceived of it in one moment in a sequence of moments which hardly differ from one another. Thus what is seen of it in one moment is as much a fragment of it as what we would see of an object moving rapidly

2. *The Hermetica*, Libellus XI, (1), Walter Scott translation, quoted in *Living Time*, by Maurice Nicoll (London: Vincent Stuart, 1953), chap. 5, p101.

past a narrow window. This gives us a mistaken idea of the object's real extension. What we take for its whole bulk at a given time is thus but a tiny section of its real being, which extends along the fourth dimension, over which consciousness travels like a narrow pencil of light.

If, therefore, a moment comes in which this object is destroyed, what is destroyed or ceases to be is only as much of that object as can be contained in a moment. This has no effect on this object in all its other places along the fourth dimension, in which it was known previously. The permanent reality of all individual times can also be seen from the fact that the reality of what exists in the present moment is not affected by its being 'past' from the point of view of the following moments. Personal identity is therefore based on a unique structure of place-time combinations, each one of which is itself unique. Not only are we invisible as spiritual beings, by far the greater part of our physical being is also invisible because only an element of it can be visible at any one time.

The principle that the combination of spatial and temporal determinations fixes things for ever is what is implicit in the Hermetic texts. Thus everything we have ever been and done must remain where it was, down to the smallest detail, and not just as a series of separate states, as memory is liable to depict it. This permanence of all being underlies the literal truth of the Koranic teaching that at the end of the world, 'whoever has done an atom's weight of good will see it, and whoever has done an atom's weight of evil will see it.'

At the same time, this clearly accounts completely for the Medieval idea that the resurrection body comprises the same material as it has now. This restitution or reintegration does not require the least particle to be taken back from anywhere, but only the cessation of the temporal flux which fragments our self-awareness. Death, or what we call the end of life, could thus only be the end of a person in the way that the last page of a book is the end of the book. If we keep to the view that the self is destroyed at death, it would still amount only to the destruction of the last point on a line composed of innumerable such points.

The Possibility of Redemption

Since the fourth dimension is as continuous as those of space, all our past momentary selves in both their mental and physical states form a single continuous organism with what we are now. This is why our present psycho-corporeal state is in dialogue with all we have been before. Not only do our past states of being directly affect our present state, this continuity means that what we do and choose now must have its effects directly on the meaning of all our previous states. That we can and do alter our own past for good or ill has always been understood in a moral sense, but this means that we do so in a natural sense as well. Otherwise, the religious idea of redemption would be confined to just one part of one's life, with no objective power over the previous life.

It also confers an additional objective reality on the psychoanalytical practice of getting in touch with one's self as it was in earlier times when it suffered some trauma. We can assume that the present state of the self can thus heal earlier ones because they really exist in union with what we are now. The ontological continuity of past, present, and future in the individual has its counterpart in the collective being of mankind. This means, among other things, that the redemptive mission of revealed religion can on this basis be extended backwards to humanity in pre-Christian and pre-Islamic times. The Christian belief in the harrowing of hell shows that this idea is admitted by tradition.

In view of its fourth-dimensional extension, our psycho-corporeal being must in reality be an extremely extended object, and for this reason Nicoll claims that the ancient Egyptians assimilated it to the serpent Apophis, which they depicted as weaving its coils in a region between Isis and Osiris. This image implies that the extension of the real self is not likely to be a straight line, but that it is in any case of enormous length. As to which form it should take, an answer is given by Guénon in *The Symbolism of the Cross*, where he describes the individual being as a system of spirals which develop both in the horizontal and the vertical.

However, Nicoll does not draw the conclusion that this linear-type extension is owing only to our present temporal condition. In reality, it is our true objective being, which the passage of time only allows us to perceive in minimal amounts. While this allows new possibilities to be realized without directly impinging on what has gone before, this comes at the expense of conscious wholeness. When physical life ends, so also must the uprooting process of time, so that there would no longer be any reason for the self to be quantitatively extended. All the apparently separated states of the self should then be capable of conscious intercommunion, quite apart from the ongoing life of the disembodied soul.

Even though the soul may subsequently be embodied with a different kind of matter from that of this life, so as to have a 'spiritual body', the latter must still be continuous with the body of this life by the mediation of the immortal soul. It is still the identity of the soul which is the cause of the bodily form, whether at a moment or through the fourth dimension. Where he relates immortality to eternal recurrence, however, there is an inconsistency in Nicoll's thought, where he writes as though the end of a person's life must mean that that person is free to re-commence and relive it, if they had not realized their true purpose.

The confusion here is between the life to be lived and the person who is to live it. According to the four-dimensional conception, the permanently subsistent life and the person who has lived it are one and the same thing. What we call the completed life is the sum total of all the person's being, as a single organism extending from conception to death. To speak of the person as though he or she could live the same life over again is as absurd as to suggest that they could separate from their own natures, like fire from its heat, or water from its moisture; there is in reality no break between the self-as-agent and its manifestations.

Nicoll states that 'man repeats his period independently of the period of manifestation of the aeon of the world,'[3] and that 'Man lives his life again,'[4] although this is to confuse the objective life with a subjective appreciation of it. In one sense we constantly relive our lives simply in the living of them, because what we do now is secretly

3. *Living Time*, chap. 8, p169.
4. Ibid., p165.

revising all we have done before. But if a literal reliving of a life was possible, it would be futile if it were an identical repetition, not least because it would be a duplication of something which was in any case permanent.

The state which follows upon the end of natural life, then, is no longer a temporal extension, but a restitution of our present mode of being, many times enriched. The supposed memory of the whole past life which some people experience when in mortal danger is therefore not really memory, because it is the life itself which is becoming manifest for a while. Memory becomes irrelevant when the whole life is all present at once, since it is necessary only to counter the passage of time while time is passing. It could be said that in heaven, memory is swallowed up in reality, as in the verse quoted by Thomas Taylor:

> There in the sight of Jove, the parent king,
> Th' immortal gods and mortal men reside
> With all that ever was, and shall hereafter be.[5]

However, the orthodox teaching is that the Judgement comes after death, but how is this to be understood in the light of what has just been described? If mortal life concludes with an everlasting body, and develops into a body with supernatural powers, it may seem that death would be pure gain for everyone. The objection to this is that the extension of the self in the fourth dimension on earth is not bound to proceed in any particular direction. The very idea of extension necessarily implies direction at the same time. Its 'qualitative direction' depends on the will, which in man is at any given time the integral sum of his physical, emotional and intellectual propensities.

On the one hand, his will may be directed to God, its First Cause, by aligning itself with Providence, where Providence comprises the revealed will of God, together with the archetypal form of the individual which is the goal of his personal development. In this way, the development of the self will lead to integration with the archetypal Form which it was his or her purpose to realize in this life. The

5. *Ten Doubts Concerning Providence*, 10, Thomas Taylor translation, from 1816 edition of *The Theology of Plato*.

significance of Forms of individuals is that they are man's only points of entry into the realm of eternal realities. Where Plato says that those who have lived well return to their own star, the star in this context corresponds to the Form of the individual.

On the other hand, these possibilities imply their converse, unfortunately, because the permanence of the person in the fourth dimension results from the physical conditions of existence, and not from its relation to Providence. If the self develops in a direction which is dictated only by natural conditions, and not by its archetypal Form, it will not have the necessary basis for any relation to God. This would result in an immortality which was deprived of the power to realize itself in the realm of the spirit, such that it could not either truly be or cease to be. The will would remain fixed on what is finally revealed to be an impossibility, while it is no longer able to change direction. As long as we are in time, this danger can be ignored, because the temporal condition veils so much from our awareness.

The impossibility of change for the will in the hereafter results from the fact that it is only in this world that the natural life can be accumulated in a given direction. The cessation of time for the individual, even if it were to be a moment without sequel, would still be quite other than what physical death appears to be. It would mean a summation and integration of innumerable states of being whose relations to one another and to God may have been ignored. The self as a whole is invisible, for the reason already given, from whence comes the possibility of delusion about the self. As death can occupy only a few such moments, its impact on the whole being can only be mental and moral, but not physical, inasmuch as it cannot affect the physical reality of the life as a whole. While there is nothing to prevent the continuation of this being outside time, its destiny depends on how much the final summation of its temporal states corresponds to its archetype.

Man's Cosmic Role

If such be the case with the death, resurrection, and judgement of the individual, the same things must also apply to the whole cosmic order. When the world ends, all animal, vegetable, and inanimate beings will also be released from their temporal dismemberment. The passage of time, which was the medium of their development, is at the same time the cause of this apparent dismemberment into a series of separate though similar bits which all seem to perish, as with human life. For this reason, the General Judgement will mean the reintegration of all beings in their fully-realized natures.

For the irrational creation, its adequacy to its archetype is not in doubt, since only human beings can fail in this respect. This is simply the compensating penalty for the human position as the supreme part of creation, with its power of self-determination and self-creation for good or ill; to have the highest place is to have the obligation of making oneself worthy of it. This, then, is in outline the answer to questions as to what must become of the non-human creation in the hereafter. The non-human creation can thus be understood as part of the 'furniture' of Heaven, so to speak.

The human power of self-determination has its implications for the whole of creation, as well as for the individual, since the human state is in virtual contact with everything else in creation. This is why the spiritual regeneration of each person has a regenerative effect on nature as a whole, while our failure in this respect has a dissolving effect on it. Thus it would be logical for the end of the world to be a time of the greatest delusion and sin, as the Book of Revelation indicates. The means for realizing this cosmic role for mankind lies in the way in which each soul is a world, which is always centered on the body, the body being the unique instantiation of the soul.

The Hermetic precept to envisage not only all the states of one's own life, but the states of the world before and after it, serves to awaken this awareness of the individually-perceived world as in some sense an extension of the self: 'I am no longer an object colored and tangible, a thing of spatial dimensions; I am now alien to all this, and to all that you perceive when you gaze with bodily eyesight,'[6] and I 'behold the Universe and myself in The Mind.'[7] This means freedom from the common sense identification of oneself

6. *Hermetica*, Libellus XIII, Walter Scott tr., (Solos Press).

7. Ibid.

with what is outwardly observable, matching the vast extension of the personal self with that of its world.

In this text, a wider union with the non-ego is added to that of all the component states of the ego, referred to before. Philosophy has expressed this universal identification as the mind's ability to recognize that its nature is to contain a representation of the world from a unique point of view. But however expressed, the point of this concept is that the alienation of the cosmos from the larger self can be overcome. Such a teaching can be seen to correspond, as Nicoll points out, to what is taught by St Paul in the Epistle to the Ephesians, and elsewhere. For example, he wishes Christians to have the power 'to comprehend with all the saints what is the breadth and length and height and depth . . . that you may be filled with all the fullness of God.'[8] This follows from the nature of the Church which, as the Mystical Body of Christ, is 'the fullness of him who fills all in all.'[9]

St Paul's explanation as to how this conscious fullness of being is to be brought about is inseparable from a conscious relationship with Christ, while the idea of cosmic identity expressed in the Hermetica appears as a consequence of an understanding of the individual's sensory world as a manifestation of his larger self. In this way, it is a possibility we can verify for ourselves. We have as much, and more, reason to identify with this larger sphere of realities as we have to identify with the tiny sphere of the ego and its desires and aversions. All things that are determinations of our consciousness have an equal right to be constituents of our identity, but the freedom we have in the way we relate to them must respect the purposes for which they were created.

The penalty for this freedom is that human beings alone in nature can represent reality as other than what it must be, and invert the order of priorities between the objective and the subjective. Sin ignores the difference between the self and the not-self, that is, between one's whole being and its ego. The commonest way in which this can happen is where means are made into ends. In this way, pseudo-ends fill the place which should belong to the real ends of life.

8. Eph. 3:18–19.

9. Ibid., 1:23

The ability to misrepresent reality is an inevitable consequence of the ability to represent it, which is essential to man's state of being.

All this is a complete contrast to the common sense way of regarding the self and the world, for which only the ego of the moment is identified as self, and everything else is seen as alien. While the ego is much over-valued, it perceives itself at the same time as adrift in an alien world which is indifferent to it, and which will ultimately destroy it. Thus the momentary physical self seems to be all the reality we have, and it prompts us to over-value it as a compensation for the way in which it is seen to be dwarfed by its world. Obviously, this elementary idea of personal identity is not untrue in itself, since it answers to facts which are easily verifiable, but by itself it is so incomplete and one-sided that it can only be a cause of conflict outwardly and despair inwardly.

However, the ego can be transformed when integrated with the higher and invisible self through which identification is possible with all past states of being, and with innumerable other realities of the represented world. In short, the world experienced as within the self is the necessary counterpoise to the natural and commonplace experience of the self as an item contained in the outside world.

The idea of our whole past life being always really present, and awaiting us after death, can cause quite different reactions. Some may find it consoling, and others may find it appalling, since it is necessarily a test of the way in which one's life has been used. But no matter how threatening it may appear to some, this conception also implies that while physical facts cannot be altered, their meaning always can be. The meaning and value of things past is changed or confirmed by the way in which we live now. Nothing is irrevocable, since it never ceases to be in contact with the activity of the self at the present time and with its deepening relation to God. To live with this enlargement of being is also to 'put on Christ' as St Paul calls it, and that must mean a certain share in the transcendence of time which is affirmed of Christ in the Easter liturgy, where it says:

> Christ yesterday, and today; the beginning, and the end; Alpha and Omega; all time belongs to him; and all the ages; to him be glory and power through every age and for ever. Amen.

Index

Index

www.ingramcontent.com/pod-product-compliance
Lightning Source LLC
Chambersburg PA
CBHW021504090426
42739CB00007B/465

* 9 7 8 1 5 9 7 3 1 0 5 6 7 *